CLEAN SLATE

By Sean Stormes

How Purpose Ignites Profit

Third Door Publishing

CLEAN SLATE

Published by Sean Stormes
Copyright © 2017 by Sean Stormes

All rights reserved. No part of this publication may be reproduced, stored, or transmitted in any form or by any means, electronic, mechanical, photocopying, recording, scanning, or otherwise, except as permitted under Section 107 or 108 of the 1976 United States Copyright Act, to include "fair use" as brief quotation embodied in articles and reviews, without the prior written permission of the author and publisher.

Limit of liability/disclaimer of warranty: The author has made every effort to ensure the accuracy of the information within this book was correct at time of publication. The author does not assume and hereby disclaims any liability to any party for any loss, damage, or disruption caused by errors of omissions, whether such errors or omissions result from accident, negligence, or any other cause. No warranty may be created or extended by sales representatives, promoters, or written sales materials. The advice and strategies contained herein may not be suitable for your situation. You should consult with a professional where appropriate. Neither the publisher nor author shall be liable for any loss of profit or any other commercial damages, including but not limited to special, incidental, consequential, or other damages.

Also by Sean Stormes

David Thompson: Skywalker (2003)

Exit Ramp (2008)

Praise for CLEAN SLATE

Tucker Trotter, CEO, Dimensional Innovations

"I was referred to Sean by another CEO, and at our first meeting we decided to engage fully. Our company had experienced good quarters and not so good quarters; good years and not so good years. I told Sean that we wanted off the roller coaster, needing more consistent profitable growth performance. Sean's work with the leadership team and me was enlightening, and I'll just say – we've never seen results like this! Now, 'We liberate people from mediocre experiences,' and it drives all that we do. Sean is a master on the subject of profitable revenue growth (PRG), just be prepared to attack it in ways you've never imagined."

Tim Cowden, President and CEO, Kansas City Area Economic Development Council

"Sean did a phenomenal job of connecting with our group of 330+ investors during his keynote presentation at our Q2 Full Council Investor Briefing. I highly recommend his purpose-driven, demand creation philosophy and framework for small and large businesses alike!"

Scott Wesley, Principal, ArrivedOutdoors

"I had been successful in business development for years, but then I heard Sean speak about Purpose and how it's the linchpin to demand creation, growth and profitability. That sounded good to me! Before I knew it, Sean helped me 'see what I'd been missing,' and ArrivedOutdoors was born. Now, it's not about selling – it's about attracting. I couldn't recommend Sean more highly, and have introduced him to my network of CEOs and business owners. Amazing!"

Sam Meers, EVP, Health and Finance, Barkley

"Smart, articulate and a treasure trove of new and progressive ideas are just a few of the ways I would describe Sean Stormes. Sean is a firm believer that what drives a business to consistent and sustainable profitable growth success is demand creation – beginning with all-important purpose. Sean has the unique ability to not only see the trees, but also to back away to see the forest. 'Seeing what others miss' is a basic tenet to Sean's magic. If you have the opportunity to work with Sean, please don't pass it up. You will experience a mutually beneficial learning experience."

Ron Hill, Founder and CEO, Redemption Plus

"Sean Stormes is a true mentor who sees the future of business. His insight, wisdom, curiosity and willingness to challenge the status quo can turn any business into a purpose-driven entity that changes the world. After 10 years in business and rapid top line growth, we struggled for a bottom line to match. Then Sean introduced me to profitable revenue growth! It just made so much sense when he talked about W. Edwards Deming, continuous improvement, demand creation, ethnography and 'Purpose before Profit.' It all clicked with me, and now we are living it! Sean has helped Redemption Plus transform from a sales organization into a value creation organization aligned around our True North (purpose). Sean helped us see the light and co-design the path to get there."

Dedication

While Clean Slate was five years in the making, its roots go back to the 1970s.

Therefore, I'd like to thank my heroes, each a renegade disruptor in their own right. While I didn't recognize the slow boil at the time, these gutsy, fearless revolutionaries shaped a progressive, game-changing mindset that finally manifested itself into what you see in these pages. To Pistol Pete Maravich, George Lucas, Eddie Van Halen, Stephen King, Steven Spielberg and Ronald Reagan: I owe each of you the high courage it took for me to not only be different, but to "pick a fight" within a stale, insipid industry in the name of "a better way."

Additionally, this section would not be complete without recognizing my mentors, the brave souls who helped me cross the chasm from conventional executive to aggressive Demand Creator. Sam Meers, Grant Gooding, Al Eidson, Brett Gibson, Sam Burke, Nate Orr, Shawn Polowniak, Kevin Koster, John Koster, and others I'm sure who contributed to the Revenution … thank you so much from the bottom of my heart because I truly owe you so much.

Regarding mentors, a very special shout out goes to my friend, former boss of 20 years, and #1 teacher extraordinaire, Roger Payne. Without you, Roger, none of this would have happened. Thank you for always having the utmost confidence in me. To say that you have had profound influence on my worldview, attitude and behaviors would be the understatement of the century.

Then there are the all-important customers who took a chance on me, and something totally new, beginning the winter of 2008-09 – breathing life into The Third Door, my profitable growth consulting firm. An oversized, gracious "thank you" to Grisel Wiley, Tucker Trotter, Joe Roetheli, Chris Larson, Scott Wesley, Gregg Davidson, Ron Hill, Paul Buchanan, Shawn Miller, Marty Bicknell, Brian O'Regan, Andrew Bash, Tim Cowden and Mike Maddox. And I would be remiss to not honor Managing Editor Russell Gray of the Kansas City

Business Journal – who awarded me a bi-monthly growth strategies column that reached thousands of business leaders each month when some thought I was a kook – and Ed Stych, Editor – Digital Cities, American City Business Journals, who took "The Little Column That Could" out to 43 of the nation's largest markets. Thank you, gentlemen, as none of this would have been possible without you.

As my demand creation journey evolved, I am forever indebted to the "big names," including Steve Jobs, Bernadette Jiwa, Seth Godin, Tim Brown, Elon Musk, Walt Disney, Tony Hsieh, Dan Cathy, Jerry Murrell, Yvon Chouinard, Reed Hastings, John Lasseter, Herb Kelleher and all of the other demand creators worldwide. I am in daily awe of how you constantly see what others miss, and what you have intentionally designed as a result. In my book (pun intended), inspiration always trumps motivation.

Last, but most importantly, I want to thank my patient and amazing wife, Susan, for her undying belief and support of this endeavor. While I toiled away evenings and weekends, she made due without me. Your sacrifice contributed to the success of this book as much as anything else. I love you, sweetheart. We did this together!

Table of Contents

Also by Sean Stormes i

Praise for CLEAN SLATE iii

Dedication vii

Introduction: Demolition of How Things Used To Be 1

Section I Takedowns 9

    Chapter 1 Anemia: 11 Causes of Poor Profitable Revenue Growth (PRG) 11

    Chapter 2 Source Code: Baseball's Powerful One-Two-Three Punch Provides Answers 37

    Chapter 3 Systems: Wise Old Sage & The Power of Harnessing Variation 53

    Chapter 4 Surrogate: The Only Reason the Sales Organization Exists (and it's not good) 79

Section II The Intentional Design of Organizational Fitness .. 107

    Chapter 5 Steam: Engineering the Unbeatable Advantage 109

    Chapter 6 Truancy: The Missing Ingredient That Dooms Most PRG Efforts 115

    Chapter 7 Linchpin: Got Purpose? (Part I) 123

    Chapter 8 "Do": More Powerful Than Values 129

    Chapter 9 Wisdom: Choosing the Most Effective Game Plan 139

    Chapter 10 Culpable: Accountable Execution 147

Section III The Seven Components of Demand Creation 155

    Chapter 11 Component One: Got Purpose? (Part II) .. 157

Chapter 12   Component Two: The Village People 167

Chapter 13   Component Three: Monopoly, Anyone?...... 181

Chapter 14   Component Four: Designing "Priceless" 193

Chapter 15   Component Five: Proceed With Caution.... 215

Chapter 16   Component Six: Captivation 223

Section IV   Sustainability 233

Chapter 17   Ethnographer Rising: The Salesperson's New Role 235

Chapter 18   Reporting: New Metrics, Measurements and Dashboards 249

Chapter 19   Building the PRG All-Star Team: Organizational Chart Redesign 257

Chapter 20   Full Integration: Baking the New Model Into The Company's Bones 273

Chapter 21   Cold Turkey: Seven PRG-Destroying Activities to Cease Immediately 281

Appendix "A" 289

About the Author 305

Introduction: Demolition of How Things Used To Be

Many companies are stuck in a growth rut, a type of business quicksand where escape has proven troublesome. That occurs because what got them "here" won't get them "there." The rules for prosperity have changed, and an overhaul of how leadership believes profitable revenue growth (PRG) occurs is not only necessary, it is required for survival in the third millennium.

Adding fuel to the fire, in America you are either a small business or you are not. Have you noticed that most business books, popular articles, and even television and news shows are focused on the technology sector, often aimed at the Fortune 500 or small business, including startups? Where can existing, *mid-market leadership* find wisdom and assistance that helps them succeed? Their challenges are much different than the aforementioned large and small business categories.

This is important to consider because the United States government offers a plethora of programs to "small business." While the federal government does not formally recognize a mid-market category, other sources do provide guidelines. This crucial segment, consisting of approximately 197,000 U.S. companies, is defined by the Small Business Administration as employing less than 200 people and generating less than $25.5 million in annual revenue. To further muddy the waters, the National Center for the Middle Market (NCMM) at The Ohio State University Fisher College of Business – one of the leading sources of research on issues of interest to U.S. midsize companies – claims that a mid-market business generates between $10 million and $1 billion per year in annual revenue. The Center also estimates that mid-market firms account for about one-third of private sector jobs *and* gross domestic product, an approximate measure of the U.S. economy after removing government spending. Furthermore, mid-market companies were the only category that experienced a net increase in jobs between 2007 and 2010, during the Great Recession.

In my four decades of business, primarily leading Sales and Marketing organizations (important to know for later), here's what I witnessed countless times: Mid-market executives read about big company "success factors" – that is *if* they read – then become frustrated because scaling those success factors to their smaller size is difficult, if not impossible. The successful, sustainable execution of what made sense on the page or screen proves much harder when similar, necessary resources are non-existent.

Regarding the overabundance of well-intending startup content, this information is often dismissed because most in the mid-market category believe it does not apply to them. The business owner crows, "We've been in business 17 years. We're not a startup!"

By contrast, the book you are holding aspires to provide a PRG blueprint for the majority of American businesses that fall in the oh-so-important "middle" (though the architecture works wonders with startups and larger firms, too). In other words, if you are looking for a book steeped in traditional competitive advantage, marketing, branding and (especially) sales tactics, put this one back on the shelf.

I am driven by a singular purpose – the difference I'm trying to make in people's lives: *"To help senior leadership create extreme customer demand and profitable growth."* The way to accomplish that feat is to arm CEOs and business owners with a proven PRG model designed specifically for the third millennium. As you will learn, I have no doubt that leadership has lost their way, even though there are occasional shining examples of "business done right." Still, it is within our core where the battle is being lost. My firm – The Third Door – is working diligently to reverse that trend.

As you begin this journey, please understand that what I am after most is your *belief system*. Beginning with Chapter One, the usual suspects – including sacred cows; protected interests; best practices; and the like – are attacked relentlessly in the name of forming a new, more relevant and higher-ROI belief system. The approach here is blunt, aggressive and provocative. I have learned through my senior level experience and daily consulting practice that this is often the only way to get the attention of willful leaders – the kind who will lead our nation back to global prosperity.

And so I ask you, curious, humble and ambitious leader: Do you believe that you can experience similar results as the following iconic companies, businesses that perform at a consistent high level of performance regardless of economic market conditions?

Southwest Airlines   Wegman's   Zappos
Starbucks   Five Guys Burgers & Fries   Costco
Chick-fil-A   Patagonia   Apple
Quick Trip   Whole Foods Market   Pixar

If you do not believe that their success can also be yours, then why? Would it help you to know that each employs similar thinking and methodology to achieve the marketplace distinction they enjoy, and that this new "source code" can be obtained and downloaded within any company where Level 5 Leadership[1] is evident?

Furthermore, do you believe that forging a monopoly – yes, I said *monopoly* – is entirely possible? Keeping in mind that your competitors are your best allies (because they will rarely, if ever, change), how hard do you think it is to perpetually uneven the competitive playing field? As Peter Thiel and Blake Masters stated so eloquently in their book, *Zero to One*, creating monopolies should be leadership's sole endeavor. Thiel and Masters make unconventional statements like, "Competition is for losers," and, "If it has to be marketed or sold, then it's not good enough." How do you feel about that? And while the subtitle of their fine book is, *Notes on Startups, or How to Build the Future*, I would like to deliver some good news:

---

[1] Jim Collins, *Good to Great*; Level 5 Leadership defined as humble yet willful leaders.

> **Clean Slate Wisdom:** Any company – with the "right" leadership – can disrupt their marketplace and design a monopoly, often within two years or less.

It is maddening and a bit sad to watch deserving companies often "put the cart before the horse," investing scarce, hard-earned money with outside resources including sales trainers; marketing, branding and advertising firms; and management consultants before first ensuring that they have something valuable to sell, market, brand, advertise or manage. In other words, in every situation I have been involved with across hundreds of companies, their products and services suffered from a severe case of "sameness," the business disease that has reached epidemic proportions.

If you purposefully design-test-improve the core business right from the start – "the tip of the spear" – all of those traditional after-the-fact solutions will be intentionally baked into the product or service, eliminating costly waste and rework. And, armed with a belief system that any company can use to transform into something much more than their industry status quo, miracles can and do happen.

Having had first-hand exposure in the late 1980s and early 1990s to American quality and productivity legend Dr. W. Edwards Deming, the man often cited as teaching the Japanese how to become the economic juggernaut they are today, I learned that before any solutions should be considered for tough problems, we should first and always consider the *causes* of the problem. Only then can we begin to understand the systemic factors that produce current and past results, and subsequently identify any inherent flaws to the system.

With these foundational thoughts in mind, I personally welcome you to *Clean Slate*, and am hopeful that you will find the answers you have been searching for. After all, the first thing a business needs is profitable, repetitive, revenue-producing customers, and that outcome serves as the basis for this book.

Thank you for your consideration, and let us begin.

Section I

Takedowns

Chapter 1

Anemia:

11 Causes of Poor Profitable Revenue Growth (PRG)

"Where ignorance is bliss, 'tis folly to be wise"

~ Thomas Gray, Poet

"The frog does not die because of the slow boil. It perishes because of brainlessness."

~ Sean Stormes

PRG is the lifeblood of business. When it is on life support, the enterprise is at risk. Operations, Finance, HR and all of the other departments become jobless if revenue evaporates.

Therefore, it is important to be aware of The Slippery Business Death Slope.

1. Exposure. Known as the silent killer, no alarms sound when new marketplace forces reposition a company for the worse. Business continues as usual, providing a false sense of security. Meanwhile, the threat grows.

2. Vulnerability. The volume and frequency of sales opportunities, not to mention subsequent revenue performance, begin a gradual, downward trend. Leadership writes off the poor performance to any number of traditional causes, refusing responsibility. Internal tensions mount as the well runs dry. Grasping at straws, leadership tries anything and everything to stem the tide, only making matters worse by increasing variation. Confusion and frustration reign while nothing seems to strike the genuine customer chord.

3. Irrelevance. Customer apathy emerges, emotionally cutting ties with the brand. In business, unlike maritime protocol, the captain rarely goes down with the ship. Self-survival becomes paramount, exit plans are identified and executed, leaving the remaining crew to search for imaginary lifeboats.

4. Obituary. There is no wake or funeral, just an empty parking lot overrun by weeds and headstones ("Out of Business"). Sadly, in most cases the carnage could have been prevented.

If you need examples to validate The Slippery Business Death Slope, pick your poison. Each of these companies is either dead, dying or has faced certain death and was purchased by another company:

Eastman Kodak   Montgomery Ward   Reebok

Circuit City   MySpace   Blockbuster   Sears

Metro Goldwyn Mayer   Time Magazine

Maxwell House   Zenith   Firestone   Merrill Lynch

Radio Shack   JC Penny   K-Mart

The combination of The Great Recession, ever-increasing choices and dynamic technology has exacerbated the Death Slope. Lazy, legacy businesses and industries are especially vulnerable in the third millennium.

Chief Value Architects – CVAs – are needed now more than ever.

For insight into how U.S. businesses have arrived at such a perilous PRG juncture, please review the following 11 causes of this anemia.

1. Top management is Stumped

Once per week, often during lunch hour, I visit Barnes and Noble, perusing new business books and magazines to gain a flavor for trending topics.

In October 2009 I spent such a lunch hour when I spied the most recent *Inc. Magazine*. From the cover, a highlighted article grabbed my attention: "The Truth About Profits," by contributing editor Darren Dahl. *Profits?* I wondered. This was the height of the aforementioned recession, and companies were actually experiencing profits? Intrigued, I bought a coffee, took a seat and began reading. (NOTE: The article can be found online by searching, "How To Protect Your Margins In a Downturn")

Dahl's article, complete with irrefutable evidence including graphs, numbers, PROOF – painted a mysterious picture. After digesting the information across 12 major industries, I had discerned what any astute business person would have regarding how the profiled companies were turning a profit during such dire economic times: They cut costs sharply, meaning freshly severed heads rolled down the streets of mainstream America, further worsening the country's unemployment dilemma. That tactic, while sometimes necessary, is always the easy way out.

While the profitability charts all trended upward, top line revenue graphs plummeted into the abyss. In fact, nine out of the 12 industries studied reflected this cataclysmic revenue erosion. What did this mean, profits soaring due to overzealous cost cutting while revenue decline peaked?

That was Mr. Dahl's point, "the truth about profits," and it was not lost on me. Top management knows how to cut cost all day long – they are subject matter experts in this area – but are often perplexed when it comes to creating PRG. To witness, some companies thrived from 2007 to 2010. You just have to know how to do it, i.e. execute the new source code.

Even today, Wall Street regularly hammers companies for revenue growth, and still the delivery truck is stuck in neutral, idling and unsure of what to do. I have dealt with hundreds of senior executives and it is shocking how many do not read, specifically the type of content that can remedy their PRG woes. If it does not square with an MBA education, then it is often reasoned that the advice must not be applicable. Additionally, it seems that if new ideas and concepts do not fit nicely into one of many traditional spreadsheets, then dismissal rules the day. Many in leadership do not seem to understand that the past and present do not predict the future, and that the ability to anticipate the "unspoken needs" that customers cannot yet articulate holds the key to the PRG kingdom.

Mere survival is nothing to be proud of, a bar set far too low. And, as many say, "Hope is not a strategy," so waiting for the economy to show new signs of life is not a prudent PRG plan.

2. Phantom Compass

Is your company a member of The Flavor of the Month Club, constantly changing stripes, strategies and people in hopes of improved performance? How's that working for you? A better question: Have you measured the waste and rework associated with such a chameleon-like existence? One year we're this, and the next year we're that.

Most every company I have had the pleasure of working with had an identity crisis. Sure, there may have been the requisite mission or vision statement that no one can remember and provides no meaningful utility (other than a Lucite paperweight). And company values? Another inconvenient truth: Leadership often behaves counter to the written values, not to mention employees. These tired exercises have proven to be "nice to have" versus "something we live and die by." The hypocrisy is curious, to say the least.

Determining a company's True North is no easy task, however once discovered and articulated concisely, the ROI is often instantly apparent. Every company decision and behavior can be measured against the firm's sense of purpose, streamlining all facets of the organization (streamlining = improved profitability). Both morale and performance improve, giving people something powerful and real to rally around. That is what forms the type of culture leaders desire, which becomes the ultimate advantage. A company's identity should not be "told." Rather, it should be "felt."

What you sell is not most important. What is most important is knowing who you are, what you stand for and what you *believe*.

3. The Emperor Has No Clothes

In PRG jargon, the "emperor" is a company's value proposition made to its customers. Call it a brand promise or whatever suits you, the fact remains that most of the time it is metaphorically "naked," yet few in the kingdom dare challenge the top dog. Leadership would rather believe that the company's suit of clothes is beautiful! That skewed belief provides calm, restful nights, putting the onus for PRG squarely on the shoulders of the Sales organization. How convenient. Yet this is how many businesses end up residing in Samenessville. Population: *Exploding*.

One of the first questions I ask senior leadership is, "What is your margin protection plan?" and, "What is your margin growth plan?" Most often I am met with blank stares, because they know these questions are valid, important and most of all, scary. "Scary" because they realize they do not have valid answers.

If I ask, "Tell me about your firm's value proposition," they begin explaining what they *do*, not how they positively impact their customers' profitability or give people something to believe in. Additionally I ask, "How do you warrant charging a premium?" First there is an uncomfortable pregnant pause, followed by some stammering, then finally, "Well, we don't often find ourselves in a position to charge a premium. Most often it's a price war."

And they wonder why their salespeople aren't delivering the performance they feel they so richly deserve.

PRG is the intentional outcome of a carefully constructed *unprecedented* value design process. It is time to "clothe the emperor," and that responsibility rests with CEOs and business owners, not Sales or Marketing or anyone else.

4. Leadership's Conventional Beliefs About the Sales Organization

Extensive conversations with business owners, CEOs and other high-ranking executives – including entrepreneurs and investors – yields a troubling conviction: PRG is the responsibility of the Sales force. In reality, nothing could be further from the truth.

Take it from someone who has led multiple sales and marketing organizations and hundreds of salespeople: the salesperson is hamstrung *at best*. She can only represent a value proposition that top management has designed, and as you will learn, most value propositions are frail, not powerful or significant. Therefore, no matter how hard she tries, how smart she is or how much prospects like her, she competes on an even playing field. Purchasing decisions will be price-driven, much to the chagrin of the people who placed her in this quagmire to begin with.

The situation becomes even more tangled when studies show that 57% of the time purchasing decisions is based on which salesperson they like most. Please consider the gravity of that finding. This means that almost six out of ten customers do business with your company NOT because of the value provided them, but because of the salesperson. What happens when the salesperson leaves the company, which most do within a few years of hire?

Only top management can make the changes necessary that place everyone in the organization into a position to win. Under current organizational design, most marketing and sales organizations are powerless to affect the company's value proposition that was designed by the emperor. Conversely, intentional design and reducing process variation are the hallmarks of exceptional company leadership.

Consider the radio conglomerate I was asked to meet with. Ranked #1 in a top 40 U.S. market, their advertising sales were in a prolonged slump. With eight individual station heads in the room, including the top salespeople – and with the grand poobah, their General Manager in attendance – I asked a singular question: "What is your most pressing challenge?" Expecting a formidable predicament from such a respected market leader, their unified response floored me.

"We can't seem to get appointments."

When I asked for the leading causes of not being able to secure appointments, the station heads and salespeople went silent. Fear was palpable, and when I finally led them to the truth – that they were "selling" and not providing clients something transcendent to believe in – the G.M. demanded to know The Third Door framework and how it could help them win. When I failed to deliver the answer fast enough for his liking, he huffed and puffed and stormed out of the room without even as much as a goodbye. I'm surprised the wolf didn't try to blow my house down.

Once the coast was clear, one brave station leader turned to me and said, "See what we're up against?"

The primary role of top management is one of Chief Value Architect, intentional designers of real purpose and unprecedented value.

5. Traditional Sales Guru Influence

Consider this fact: Per an extensive 2011 Miller Heiman study, 86% of salespeople do not even reach 90% of their annual sales quota, yet – per *Sales and Marketing Magazine* – U.S. companies spend over $15 billion per year on sales training. That is some crazy, funky math. It begs the question of why company leadership invests that kind of money for minimal, if any, ROI.

Enter the gurus.

When company factions outside of the sales arena – including Engineering, Finance, Research and Development, Marketing and Operations to name just a few – seek outside assistance, the options tend to be proven, credible, and possess the necessary experience, education and documented results. However, when revenue growth is required, leadership often turns to some of the most well known names in the sales training industry – high-powered firms and celebrity gurus alike (and at times industry-specific) – too many to list here though I have come to simply refer to them as "The Usual Suspects." I'm sure you can name them.

The gurus' coffers have ballooned over the years, so much so that their respective marketing machines create an omnipresence that is hard to ignore. Preying on tens of thousands of new salespeople entering the vocation each year – and company leadership who aren't knowledgeable of how PRG occurs – outrageous promises are made that drive a cult-like following to their books, seminars, workshops and corporate engagements. Back in my corporate days, I led hundreds of salespeople through these company-required trainings – with minimal to zero correlated growth – and that is partially what led to the framework you will learn in this book.

To quote the subtitle of Michael Port's best seller, *The Contrarian Effect*, "Why it pays (big) to take typical sales advice and do the opposite," I couldn't have said it better. In fact, now having proven that salespeople are not the root cause of the PRG problem – identity crisis, sameness and lack of leadership are – the sales training industry is one whose demise cannot come to soon. Stale, selfish and manipulative techniques are not what customers seek from their vendors.

Each of the aforementioned company disciplines has evolved over the past 100 years except for one: *Sales*. Now you know why. The Golden Goose is fiercely protected by deep-pocketed gurus hell bent on ensuring the survival of their lucrative charade. And since less than 100 colleges and universities nationwide offer any type of sales-related degree, just about anyone can enter the game and become guru #486. Develop a shtick and some unsuspecting salesperson or company leader may beat a path to your door.

Smoke and mirrors "Slick Willy" might put 500 butts in seats at the local Sheraton, but how many of the brainwashed attendees actually realize the results they pine for? As one popular movie made famous, "Show me the money!"

Said another way, entire companies should succeed, not just the top 3% of salespeople.

6. Leadership's Lack of Knowledge About Statistical Variation: Understanding of a "System"

It has been statistically proven that 90% of all errors, mistakes and problems are caused by the system – how the work gets done – *not the worker*. This counterintuitive truism is the basis for Six Sigma. Enlightened leaders are well aware that to increase PRG, process variation and associated waste and rework must continuously shrink.

Without getting too technical, it is therefore important to realize the impact of this fact on PRG. If the worker (salesperson) is not the problem, then we must analyze the system of how PRG occurs, identifying both the critical success factors and root causes of poor PRG, then constantly work to optimize that system. Have you successfully mapped your internal processes by department? If not, why?

In the 1999 hit movie *The Matrix*, Neo – the reluctant hero with developing powers – asks Morpheus, leader of the rebellion, "What are you trying to tell me? That I can dodge bullets?" Morpheus quietly responds, "No, Neo. What I'm telling you is that when you're ready, you won't have to."

The same concept applies in the revenue revolution. When the PRG ecosystem is understood, aligned, optimized and executed properly, you won't need to rely on such an overt, costly, long in the tooth, low-ROI sales approach executed by below average salespeople.

Company *systems* cause results, not human will. (See #3: Worthless value propositions).

7. Prostitution

When companies do not stand for something meaningful – therefore intentionally trying to "be all things to all people," accepting checks from anyone who will write one – then they exist as a gigolo.

"All business is good business" is a cataclysmic mantra. All customers are *not* created equally. Have you stratified the customer base to determine which ones are costing you the most profit dollars per sale? Additionally, salespeople, threatened to achieve monthly quotas "or else," generally possess feeble opportunity pipelines, causing them to secure any type of business they can. Rare is the company that holds the sales organization responsible for anything more than "sales dollars secured."

Imagine an environment where you have determined which industries you know best, are experts in and can provide the greatest value. Why would anyone ever let a salesperson secure new business not aligned with the pre-approved list of industries and specific categories served? I have worked with such clients, and when that happens an exception must be requested. That request gets the salesperson a not-so-enjoyable meeting with the CEO to explain why she wants to "break rank."

In the Revenution, "narrower" is more advantageous than "wider."

8. Cart Before Horse

As you will learn, out of the hundreds of possibilities there are only a few crucial components that comprise PRG nirvana.

Leave one component out, or execute out of order, and the entire framework collapses like a house of cards.

Often, when asked to initially visit company senior management, I will ask what remedies they have previously employed to solve their PRG problems. The most frequent answers range from sales training (like it's the sales team's fault; the same group that was rewarded with a trip to the Bahamas two years ago); market research (big dollars; rarely helps); and my all-time favorite, the website or brand refresh (big dollars again; often ineffective; known as "re-skinning" or putting lipstick on a pig).

I then print the prospect's website home page and those of their top five competitors (company names blacked out). When the website refresh answer comes, the printouts are provided. "What do you notice?" I ask. Leadership answers, "They all look the same." I reply, "That's true. Can you identify yours?" Almost always, someone will choose a competitor's example. At this point they realize the money they have wasted. Here's a secret: Some executives point out that the competing firm's *logos* look the same. Ouch! How's that for trying to gain notice and marketplace distinction?

Why and how does this happen, you ask?

Top management believes that what already exists at their company is "just" and screams real competitive advantage, so the next logical step is to amplify their secret sauce to the stratified customer base, instructing the sales force to "Go get 'em!" The problem is the emperor actually has no clothes, and turning up the volume on the hollow value proposition achieves the exact opposite of the original intention: Sameness blaring across all communication channels, further thrusting the firm into customer apathy hell.

Be wary of launching marketing or sales efforts without substantial meat on the bone, the type that drives lucrative lions, tigers and bears to your doorstep – hungry eyes lusting for your offerings.

Please remember, *the only reason the sales organization exists is because demand does not.* Therefore, the objective is to design, develop and create demand before doing anything else.

9. The Mirror Effect

No matter how many times we've heard, "It's not about you, it's about them – the customer!" the problem persists. In fact, it's worse than ever. "Curio-empathy," the powerful combination of curiosity and empathy, is in severe shortage across many American boardrooms and sales organization leadership.

All too often what permeates companies is a myopic self-affirmation of greatness. Instead, leadership should focus on critical *systemic* components that include employees, customers, influencers and vendors.

People stop in their tracks when, while delivering keynote speeches, I pause, change tone and declare, "If you want to double your business in the next 12 months, *stop selling*." Stunned, there is palpable silence. "Start helping people instead. Help them by surprising with products, services and experiences they haven't yet conceived and that deliver unprecedented value. Champion new truths and belief systems. Give them a reason to love you."

Shouldn't business be more than one big, selfish money grab? If you answer 'yes,' then what does the alternative look like? How will you help people get better, faster and stronger? How will you help them fulfill *their* purpose, fortify *their* competitive advantages and help delight *their* customers?

10. Old School Mentors

I once wrote an American City Business Journals column about C-level peer-to-peer organizations and how they occasionally let their members down. This was not conjecture on my part. I reported what executives shared with me.

Within 12 hours of publication, the CEO of one of the most well known organizations in that industry sniffed around my LinkedIn profile, most likely wondering, "Who is this schmuck trying to expose us for who we really are?" Paranoia was evident. Talk about an indictment! I never named names, so why did he assume I was talking about *his* organization?

Examples abound. One day after a particular speech, I was conversing with a few of the attendees. There were four of us in a circle – three business owners and myself – while two others waited patiently off to the side to engage: a new salesperson and her manager. The moment there was a lull, sales manager guy barged into the circle, hand extended to one of the owners. "I'm Jim from (payroll processing company). When I was with another firm, 'bout five years ago, I sent you a proposal tryin' to get your business. Remember?" The owner, eyebrow raised, replied, "Not really."

Undeterred, sales manager guy plunged forward. "That's OK. Say, how about I shoot you a quote next week?

I'll bring it over myself!" Talk about an awkward moment. Now completely annoyed, the owner said, "Call me first to schedule an appointment." Turning to his newbie salesperson learning at the master's knee, sales manager guy smiled, suggesting, *And that's how it's done, honey.* When sales manager guy and his rookie left, I turned to the owner and asked, "Will you speak with him?" The owner replied, "Not on your life."

I felt bad for the rookie on many different levels.

These old-fashioned dinosaur sales mentors keep the vicious cycle turning in perpetuity, brainwashing innocent newbies to follow their archaic, low-ROI lead. There is precious little personal investment or development, and if the "numbers" aren't met, out comes the hammer. The dinosaurs believe that salespeople are expendable, never considering the tremendous waste and rework costs associated with keeping the revolving door, merry-go-round adequately staffed. And it may be worst in the real estate, financial services and insurance industries, where throwing as many newbies against the wall as possible, to see who survives, is the norm.

In fact, wherever you find a company or industry where most of the employment risk is placed more on the salesperson than the company – think transportation (gas, vehicle maintenance); paperwork administration; sales meeting time; and the like – I'll show you a business that not only suffers from sameness, but also one that cares more about greed than it does about people, and that includes customers.

11. Unaware of What People Really Buy in the Third Millennium

In 2012 and 2013, Cadillac's cars reflected high quality, but low sales (globally). On the other hand, per formal studies, BMW's similar automobiles reflected *lesser* quality yet enjoyed *much higher* sales volume. How can this be?

Consider that Apple's iPhone – made with similar components as other smart phones – commands a 70% price premium, even with many consumer advocates stating that rival phones are "better." In fact, one 2015 study estimated that the iPhone enjoyed 92% of all smartphone profits. And how to explain Tim Tebow, easily one of the least proficient quarterbacks in NFL history, who often claimed the league's highest selling jersey? As if that's not enough, did you know that the iconic rock band KISS is generally regarded as being musically average (at best), yet is one of the highest selling, most profitable bands of all time?

Could it be that quality, (claimed) differentiation and traditional benefits that address "known pain points" are not what compel people to buy? If that is true, what is it that trips people's buying triggers?

Chapter 2

Source Code:

Baseball's Powerful One-Two-Three Punch Provides Answers

"Common sense gets a lot of credit that belongs to cold feet"

~ Arthur Godfrey,
American broadcaster and entertainer

"If you want the system to deliver different, 'better' results, then change the source code"

~ Sean Stormes

In the 2011 hit movie *Moneyball* starring Brad Pitt as Billy Beane, General Manager of Major League Baseball's Oakland A's, the grand old game's conventional wisdom is openly and seriously challenged for the first time. Beane, influenced by his newly acquired assistant G.M. Peter Brand – played by Jonah Hill and a composite character primarily influenced by the real life Paul DePodesta – begins valuing baseball talent in an unorthodox way, employing a heavy dose of sabermetrics versus customary observation methods used by the sport's scouts for over 100 years. (Note: The term sabermetrics is derived from the acronym SABR, which stands for the Society for American Baseball Research)

What is sabermetrics? In the 1970s, Bill James, the godfather of the discipline and responsible for coining the term, began using overlooked and in depth statistics derived from on-field play that did not appear in newspaper box scores yet proved to be valuable when determining a player's true worth – the specific contribution to winning baseball games. James was thought to be a crackpot for decades as pioneers often are. The maverick statistician railed against prevailing assumptions that player performance in the traditional areas of batting average, RBIs (runs-batted-in) and home runs were the true indicators of a batter's worth. On the pitching side, baseball purists had pointed to a hurler's number of wins, strikeouts and ERA (earned-run-average) as primary indicators that separated "best" from mediocre. James was a low-key devil's advocate, an unintentional thorn in the old guard's side, continuously honing the science of sabermetrics.

In reality, Billy Beane, with help from DePodesta and other SABR experts, executed a baseball fire sale between late 2001 and 2002, shedding high-priced though low-producing players (according to sabermetrics), signing lower-priced castoffs that provided the A's more "value" that ultimately contributed to winning more games.

Please refer to the following facts to gain a more comprehensive perspective and understanding of what occurred with Beane's A's between the onset of the Moneyball approach in 2002 and 2012.

Oakland A's since the 2002 inception of Moneyball principles (through 2012)

- **102** wins in 2001 (lost in the American League Division Series, three games to two)
- **103** wins in 2002, the first year of Moneyball (lost in the ALDS again 3-2)
- **87** wins per season average from 2002 to 2014, 5.8% more than the American League (81.3 wins per season)
- Reached the playoffs six of those 13 years, or **46%** of the time
- Reached the **American League Championship Series in 2006** – one step away from the World Series – eventually losing to the Detroit Tigers
- **Won the A.L. West division crown in 2012** over the two-time defending league World Series entrant Texas Rangers, and the Los Angeles Angels who committed $331 million over 10 and five years respectively to new first baseman Albert Pujols and pitcher C.J. Wilson in 2011's off-season. The A's had few, if any notable

players in 2012 and a **total team (and staff) payroll of $55.4 million.**
- ➤ The A's payroll is historically and consistently one of baseball's smallest – **an average of $57.4 million from 2002 to 2012** – while their win totals from the Moneyball era are above league average (the aforementioned +5.8%)
- ➤ To contrast, the **New York Yankees averaged an annual $188 million annual payroll** from 2002 – 2012, or a 229% premium over the Moneyball A's. While the Yanks reached the playoffs 10 of the 11 years, they won the World Series just once, in 2009. **The Yankees spent $1.4 billion more than the A's during these 11 years to achieve their lone title.**

NOTE: Starting in 2015, the A's fortunes soured. It is my opinion this occurred not because Moneyball failed the A's, but the A's failed Moneyball. GM Beane began behaving like his traditional peers, chasing the high-priced free agent vs. staying true to the source code that had delivered a decade of excellence. Proof: Heading into the 2014 American League Playoffs, Beane traded for talented, expensive free agent pitcher Jon Lester, attempting to bolster his pitching staff for the post-season run, clearly an anti-Moneyball decision. The A's lost a one game playoff to the upstart Kansas City Royals, were sent home packing, and have not yet recovered as of this writing.

Boston Red Sox End "The Curse"

With the A's stellar performance in the 2000s, Beane was sure to receive some attention from other clubs. Baseball had never seen that much winning combined with such low financial investment, i.e. off-the-charts ROI.

Enter the Boston Red Sox.

After 86 years of championship futility – they hadn't won since 1918 with Babe Ruth – Boston defeated the St. Louis Cardinals in 2004 to become World Series winners. "The Curse," referring to what the Red Sox suffered through after selling Ruth to the rival New York Yankees in December of 1919, was finally broken. The Red Sox decided that championships suited them just fine in the third millennium, so they won it all again in 2007, upending the Colorado Rockies in the Fall Classic. While Red Sox owner John Henry attempted unsuccessfully to woo Beane away from Oakland in late 2002, Boston did manage to adopt the A's source code in

2003. Owner Henry hired none other than outsider and expert sabermetrician Bill James. The rest is baseball history.

In a Time magazine article from 2006 entitled, "The Time 100: Our list of the 100 men and women whose power, talent or moral example is transforming our world," here is what Mr. Henry had to say about his star employee, Bill James:

"What we now know as Moneyball and sabermetrics came from (Bill) James. He taught us, among other things, that individual ballparks have a profound effect on a ballplayer's production, that the largest variable determining how many runs a team will score is how many times the leadoff hitter gets on base, that much of what we perceive as pitching is actually defense. What I call 'Jamesian' principles infuse our thinking with a perspective that is objective rather than subjective. What James demands is that we take the time to listen to what the game is telling us over and above what we are predisposed to believe."

From the same article, then-Red Sox General Manager Theo Epstein, himself a disciple of James' teachings: "He was an outsider, self-publishing invisible truths about baseball while the establishment ignored him. Now 25 years later, his ideas have become part of the foundation of baseball strategy."

Please take a moment to reflect. *"Take time to listen to what the game is telling us over and above what we are predisposed to believe."* That loud noise you hear is the sound of centuries-old paradigms shattering. *"The establishment ignored him."* Of course they did. That's what the footsteps of obsolescence sound like, driving fear into the hearts of the sameness crowd. *"His ideas have become part of the foundation of baseball strategy."* Remember those words as you continue reading because acceptance of something new and more effective does not have to be so painful.

Pattern-breakers tend to advance the accepted source code, though change is often hard in the face of ingrained paradigms developed over long periods of time. In other words, remain in the status quo at your own peril.

Reflecting yet again, can these examples effectively and intelligently cross over into the PRG discussion? Let's first explore the "third punch" in our success equation.

Chicago Cubs End 108-year Championship Dry Spell

I have written about innovative baseball manager Joe Maddon many times in the American City Business Journals. From 2006-2014, his unconventional, player-centric leadership approach resulted in many surprising winning seasons for the lowly, cash-strapped Tampa Bay Rays.

When Tom Ricketts bought the loveable loser Cubbies in 2009 for $875 million, the first thing he did was assemble a leadership team that could deliver the club from a 108-year championship drought. First, Ricketts secured Theo Epstein from the Boston Red Sox, installing him as President of Baseball Operations. Then, Epstein in turn pried Joe Maddon away from the Rays, completing the leadership trifecta: Ricketts, Epstein and Maddon, aligned toward one purpose, to liberate the Northsiders from baseball hell.

The perfect storm, intentionally designed by Owner Ricketts from the start, occurred. The idealist owner, obsessed with a singular focus – to win the World Series. Epstein, fresh off two World Series wins in Boston (where baseball titles were non-existent prior to his arrival), hell bent on creating an all-new championship formula. And finally Maddon, the wacky, cowhide alchemist, tasked with instilling a belief system that could overcome astronomical odds.

Epstein the championship architect wanted to take Moneyball a step further, to fuse chemistry and character along with "the physical" and the analytical power of sabermetrics. The master plan also required a careful blend of veterans and rookies, with Maddon responsible for getting each to overachieve in the name of fulfilling the purpose. This step-by-step blueprint became known as "The Cubs Way," and there is a book of the same name (by Tom Verducci).

NOTE: As you continue reading, I suggest you keep separate notes creating your own "The (insert personal or company name) Way."

The Revenution: Part I

A pattern breaking "revenue revolution" – The Revenution – is the business version of Moneyball and is available to anyone who chooses to embrace its splendor.

After spending more than 27 years leading sales organizations large and small, including hundreds of salespeople and their management, I knew that there had to be a better way than what had served as a success model since the 1800s.

Sales training, cold calling, kindergarten-level performance metrics, fear, carrot dangling, the same required meetings day after day, month after month and year after year resulted in incremental growth one quarter, flat the next and stellar results yet the next. There was very little to no correlation between traditional, accepted sales behaviors and strategies, and realized PRG performance. The hairs on my skeptical neck bristled more frequently as the second millennium came to a close.

Around 2002, I snapped. *HARD.* I had accepted a regional leadership position with a global, multi-billion dollar industrial supply firm and – thoroughly disappointed with the past – was determined to try out new ideas I had developed. Eschewing the "company line," I executed a covert strategy with the sales organization, focusing on just one area that could become a real competitive advantage: Electronic sales, i.e. revenue generated via the company's new web portal where customer orders could be placed any time of day or night.

Primarily working with the top 20% of salespeople that I felt could drive 80% of results in this new focus area of electronic sales, I begged headquarters to devote corporate and regional training resources to our group first, saying that we had already embraced the new, progressive rollout (not entirely true – the salespeople didn't have a clue). Since our company was at least two years out in front of the competition, and now that our team was six months ahead of the rest of the company, we dominated this new revenue channel in 2003 and finished #2 in the nation in percentage of revenue growth year-over-year.

Why the myopic focus, and why not simply follow rote instructions like every other sales executive? I had been reading about companies that were consistently winning the PRG wars regardless of the economy's health, impervious to outside conditions that defeated their competitors. Taking copious notes during this analysis period, I had developed the beginnings of a belief system – a radical business platform – which begged for ratification.

Companies studied included but were not limited to:

- Southwest Air
- Patagonia
- UnderArmour
- Disney
- BMW
- Apple, Inc.
- Whole Foods Market
- Pixar
- and subsequently, around 2009, Zappos, Five Guys Burgers and Fries, and others we will use as shining examples throughout this book.

NOTE: There are no B2B companies listed because they tend to delegate the lifeblood of their company – PRG – to the Sales and Marketing organizations.

As of this writing, I have spent over 54,000 hours analyzing, identifying and unlocking the new source code – common "success themes" – that create a new, proven and exciting PRG blueprint for the third millennium. These critical success factors (CSFs), at times overshadowed in the PRG ecosystem by other low-ranking elements embraced by the sameness crowd, are what cause the desired results.

My hypothesis was that if these core CSFs were identified amidst the larger herd, aligned in a specific order and executed near-flawlessly without skipping any steps in the framework, then optimum PRG results would occur, often to the tune of double and triple digit top line revenue growth and substantial margin improvements.

"Take time to listen to what the game is telling us over and above what we are predisposed to believe."

I became an ardent student of PRG, relentlessly pursuing the truth which I knew had to exist. Similar to 1999's *The Matrix*, I was faced with a choice. Take the blue pill and play it safe with the sameness crowd, resulting in minimal risk, or swallow the red pill and become exposed to the truth about business in general, and specifically how PRG is designed, developed and delivered.

Similar to Billy Beane and the rock world's legion of fans, I chose the red pill. It was actually an easy decision since I had made similar choices in the past. And the most important choice lay before me in the Fall of 1988 when I was introduced to a man who would challenge my own deep seated paradigms, force my hand and set me on the path to PRG nirvana.

It was time to listen to what the game was telling me, and my teacher had no equal.

Chapter 3

Systems:

Wise Old Sage & The Power of Harnessing Variation

"A bad system will beat a good person every time"

~ Dr. W. Edwards Deming,
Professor, Author, Management Consultant

"Uncertainty, unpredictability and high costs are the byproducts of a leadership team relying on intuition instead of 'profound knowledge'"

~ Sean Stormes

In Chapter 1 we learned about the The Slippery Business Death Slope and The Eleven Causes of Anemic PRG. Since the "Emperor" – your company's value proposition – is most likely barely clothed or naked, and therefore has little chance of winning big long term, the first order of business should be to anchor the new foundation in a proven philosophy that has resulted in unparalleled global success for over 60 years. Until now it has never been so purposely and comprehensively applied to the revenue side of the profit and loss (P&L) statement, though some industry leaders we will analyze unknowingly borrow occasionally from this ideology.

We have been taught to believe that there is no one answer to business problems, no singular methodology that applies across the enterprise. "Don't put all of your eggs in one basket" remains a favorite American axiom. However, as with most concepts you will learn in this book, aphorisms like these no longer have a valid address in today's highly competitive business world. Again, what got you here won't get you there.

To fully grasp the immense power of our new, state-of-the-art foundation, and its acclaimed author, climb aboard the Revenution time machine for a brief history lesson.

Origins: Rise of a New Business Hero

Our story begins in an unlikely place: World War II.

While Nazi Germany formally surrendered to Allied Forces in May of 1945, effectively ending the war in Europe, the Pacific War raged on. Two months later the United States, in conjunction with the Republic of China, demanded Japan's surrender in the Potsdam Declaration, threatening the Japanese with "prompt and utter destruction." Emperor Hirohito and his Japanese leadership ignored the ultimatum, and two atomic bombs were dropped, the first one – dubbed "Little Boy" – on

Hiroshima (August 6), and the second – "Fat Man" – on Nagasaki (August 9). The devastation was both horrific and complete. On August 15, the Japanese raised a white flag, and then signed their Instrument of Surrender on September 2, officially ending the last World War.

On August 29, General Dwight D. Eisenhower, Supreme Commander of the Allied Forces, ordered General Douglas MacArthur to exercise authority over the Japanese government, including Emperor Hirohito. As part of MacArthur's staff that helped the proud, Eastern country rebuild and chart a new course that ultimately made them one of the world's foremost economic superpowers, the General enlisted the services of a friend in 1950 – an astute statistician and productivity expert named Dr. W. Edwards Deming.

Prof. W. Edwards Deming

During the war, Deming was part of the Emergency Technical Committee and an integral component in the compilation of the American War Standards. He taught statistical process control (SPC) to American workers engaged in wartime production, a common practice, but his proven statistical methods that optimized product quality faded in the late 1940s and 1950s as huge overseas demand for American mass-produced products materialized. "Good enough" became American business leadership's mantra, something they would regret years later.

Where, though, did Deming amass his shrewd philosophy that would eventually change the world? A 1921 graduate of the University of Wyoming at Laramie, majoring in electrical engineering, Deming also received an M.S. from the University of Colorado, and finally a Ph.D. from Yale University. Armed with graduate degrees in mathematics and mathematical physics, he worked for the U.S. Department of Agriculture, and was also a statistical adviser for the U.S. Census Bureau. Deming taught statistical theory at New York University's graduate School of Business Administration, and Columbia University's graduate School of Business, all the while consulting for private business.

In 1927, Deming was introduced to Walter Shewhart of Bell Telephone Laboratories. Inspired by Shewhart's work,

Deming adopted the concepts of SPC and control charts, and began applying Shewhart's tools to industrial production and management. The idea that good and bad process performance was *not* caused by the same set of factors – there were found to be "common" causes (random variation caused by inherent factors) and distinct "special" causes (abnormal variation due to forces outside of the normal process) – led to Deming's paradigm-busting theory of management.

Deming understood that these ideas could be applied not only to manufacturing processes, but also to processes by which enterprises are led and managed. This key insight made possible his enormous influence on the economics of the industrialized world after 1950. While Deming acknowledged Shewhart's brilliance, he worked tirelessly to make the concepts easier to understand for everyone.

In 1947, Deming was asked to assist in the planning for the 1951 Japanese census.

His expertise in quality control techniques, combined with his involvement in Japanese society, led to his receiving an invitation from the Union of Japanese Scientists and Engineers (JUSE). JUSE members had studied Shewhart's techniques, and as part of Japan's reconstruction efforts they sought an expert to teach SPC. From June–August 1950, Deming trained hundreds of engineers, managers, and scholars in the concepts of quality control. He also conducted at least one session for top management, the participants including Akio Morita, the co-founder of Sony.

Deming's message to Japan's business leadership was clear: Improving quality reduces expenses while increasing productivity, profitability, customer delight and market share. In fact, it is widely reported that in the summer of 1950, while addressing hundreds of core JUSE members, Deming made a prediction:

"If you do what you've been taught, you can become an exporting nation within five years, and can have the lion's share of any world market you desire within 25 years."

Deming felt confident making that statement because he believed that America's non-quality focus made it vulnerable. Conclusively, Deming's prediction enticed a Japanese nation decimated by war and with nowhere to go but up.

A number of Japanese manufacturers applied Deming's techniques and experienced theretofore unheard of levels of quality and productivity. The improved quality combined with the lowered cost created new international demand for Japanese products. In 1973, while the U.S. experienced a painful oil embargo, smaller, less expensive and gas-efficient cars from Japan began to gain favor. Honda, Toyota and Datsun (Nissan's predecessor) saw their respective sales spike. As the 1970s blossomed, owners rejoiced in the quality of their vehicles from the Land of the Rising Sun. The Japanese cars not only required less money to buy and less fuel, they also needed fewer repairs and didn't rust as quickly.

For anyone who believes that the 2009 Federal bailout of General Motors and Chrysler was the first of its kind, guess again. By 1979, Chrysler faced its first billion dollar annual loss. In 1980, with 200,000 U.S. jobs at stake, the smallest of Detroit's Big Three asked the White House for Federal assistance.[2] In the early 1980s, when Japanese exports began to capture more U.S. markets, America finally woke from its drunken slumber and rediscovered Deming, then in his

---

[2] *Bailout Nation: How Greed and Easy Money Corrupted Wall Street and Shook the World Economy*, by

Ritholtz, Fleckenstein, and Task

eighties. The primary catalyst was a 1980 NBC News special entitled, "If Japan Can, Why Can't We?" which featured a brief section on Deming's work. Just as he had predicted in 1950, his business model enabled the Japanese to begin exporting with success in 1952 – three years ahead of schedule – and dominating select U.S. industries by the mid-1970s.

Dr. Deming declined to receive royalties from the transcripts of his 1950 lectures, causing JUSE's board of directors to establish the Deming Prize in December of that year to repay him for his friendship and kindness. To comprehend the magnitude of the award, it is the Japanese business version of the Nobel Prize. The Deming Prize continues to exert considerable influence over the Japanese disciplines of quality control and quality management. In addition to the Deming Prize, Emperor Hirohito also awarded Deming Japan's highest civilian honor, the Second Order Medal of the Sacred Treasure, for his vital role in the rebirth of Japan's economy.

For many years there were three billboard-size pictures that hung proudly in the entryway of Toyota's world headquarters. The first was of the founder, Kiichiro Toyoda. The next depicted the current CEO. The largest photo, though, was reserved for their teacher, Dr. W. Edwards Deming.

For a small country that was once known for cheap, shoddy products that included transistor radios and dime store trinkets, the Japanese flourished under Deming's tutelage. "Made in Japan" was a derogatory statement repeated deep into the late 1960s. Today, the term connotes premium quality and luxury goods and services.

Japan's rise to economic power occurred because of one irrefutable truth: *Management's thinking had to change to achieve the results they realized.*

Good Morning, Dr. Deming

In the fall of 1988, after six years of field supervision and branch management at Yellow Freight System (now YRC Worldwide), one of the nation's top three less-than-truckload (LTL) freight haulers at the time, I was promoted to Quality Assurance Analyst in the company's Overland Park, Kansas world headquarters. It was the fourth promotion during my short tenure with Yellow, and at 27 years old, I felt pretty sure of myself.

I had worked in a region where the training and mentorship was outstanding, and my performance reflected it.

Our regional leadership team was accomplished and exceptional, and they knew it. Drinking from their respective faucets at every opportunity, I could feel myself growing personally and professionally. The awards piled up, and I knew it was time for the next chapter in my career. To work in the General Offices just outside Kansas City sounded exciting and promising, and it sure beat the diesel fumes, teamster grievances and grumbling customers I was accustomed to. I arrived in the daunting main lobby of the company's corporate offices confident (yet unsure) of what my new responsibilities entailed.

Intuitively, "Quality" seemed to mean that "Do it right the first time" would be a new corporate rallying cry. I remembered reading that somewhere. Errors and mistakes would be minimized, and customers would be happier. Confusion set in, though, because I assumed that everyone already wanted to do a good job the first time around. Ignoring that troublesome notion, one of the first pieces of business was to attend a live simulcast seminar at the local community college. The featured speaker was some really (*really*) old guy I had never heard of, however he must be good, I reasoned, because it was announced that over 4,000 people would be watching him nationwide.

After gathering coffee and exchanging pleasantries with fellow attendees, approximately 200 of us took our assigned seats. As the projected image on the theater-style screen slowly faded into view, we observed a nicely dressed, ancient turtle approaching the stage. He walked slowly and deliberately, and as he turned to face the crowd before him, the auditorium exploded into standing applause, including the one I was in. I thought, "Is Bruce Springsteen here?" The older gent – 88 at the time – flashed a brief, crooked smile, acknowledged the crowd, then politely waved everyone back to their chairs. Seated next to me was a woman wearing Donna Karan. A senior executive, I assumed. She said, "Can you believe we're actually going to learn from the master himself?" Giddy as a schoolgirl, she opened her notebook and prepared for the gospel.

"What's happening here?" I thought. "What master?" My masters were confirmed and validated, and they were back on the East coast dealing with trucks and teamsters.

Dr. Deming finally opened his mouth, and with what sounded like the voice of God himself, he asked, "What is Quality?" And with that, in his thundering, authoritative way, he proceeded to destroy every management principle I had ever been taught. To witness, I learned that 90% of all mistakes, problems and errors are caused by the system, not the employee. Internal competition destroys the company, as does ranking divisions and the people within them. Compensating based on a merit system and MBO (management by objective) were diseases to be eradicated. Understanding statistical theory, especially the concept of variation, was paramount to success. Involve front line workers, and empower them, in fact. With my belief system shattered and my mentors' manual for success drifting out of sight down a long, lonely river, I listened for hours, riveted, and was happy to do so.

My life has never been the same.

Deming scolded, encouraged, taught and warned us. He counseled on the dangers of Western Management, and that it would be wise to study our Japanese counterparts. "Quality is a function of *management*," he said. "Western leadership is severely lacking in many areas, especially in the understanding of a system." He sounded worried, like he wouldn't be around to finish what he started, to save his native land that shunned him for decades but now struggled mightily in the face of a new and fierce economic foe.

The sage turtle lectured for eight hours, only breaking briefly for lunch. "This guy's on a mission," I told a colleague. "He has more energy than I have!" As luck would have it, Dr. Deming visited the University of Kansas in Lawrence, Kansas, around 1990. To see my new hero and mentor in person remains a personal highlight. One might think that listening to a 90 year-old man blather on about statistics and admonish management hour after hour might be boring, or insane, even. To the contrary, the more I listened, read, learned and applied, every former tough business problem I'd ever faced became increasingly simple to solve.

Inspired, I made it my life's mission to learn everything I could about Deming's philosophy and methods, and how to incorporate them into whatever organization I would subsequently lead. While I'm proud to admit that for 27 years I almost always worked for an industry leader, not one of them had heard of Dr. Deming or his methods.

Frustration grew, but not before experiencing some pleasant surprises.

An Awakening

Armed with proper context and the master on my side, I now understood why my fellow leaders at Yellow Freight System often made questionable and damaging decisions. The company expanded rapidly in the 1980s and 1990s, therefore promotions – and associated higher salaries – were plentiful for top performers. Of course, my definition of a top performer had changed since Dr. Deming entered my equation.

For example, in Yellow's trucking operations, "Load Average" was a primary metric. The objective was to haul as much freight – and therefore weight – per trailer, thereby reducing the number of trailers that had to be transported, saving cost. Every facility had a load average goal, and there was hell to pay if that goal wasn't met. Often, there were daily conference calls to discuss each branch's respective key productivity and sales metrics, and if the previous day's goals were not met or exceeded, profanity flew from boss's mouths. Fear wasn't just present. It was more like the very air we breathed.

Knowing just about everyone within our 22-branch region, inevitably a random discussion would turn toward load average. When I learned that many dock supervisors would falsify a trailer's weight – easy to do by creating dummy paperwork for phantom, wayward shipments – Dr. Deming's deep, resonant voice thrummed between my ears. Sure, Yellow's top brass saw what they wanted to see: High load average sitting neatly within a box on their spreadsheet. However, true costs continued to rise because they had created a mirage.

This type of "gaming the system" occurred in just about every facet of the company's sales and operations disciplines. Occasionally there were grumblings about Yellow's slim profit margins, which were around five cents on the dollar, if that. I knew exactly what was happening, but would have been burned at the stake had anyone in senior management been told. The dirty little secrets that plagued the company had become destructive addictions, exacerbated by a leadership culture slave to MBO.

Sales goals were plucked from the sky, intended to motivate while the opposite result was almost always the case. If a branch location did $5 million in sales the previous year, the decision was to "motivate" these high performers to achieve an 8% increase, for example. With no knowledge of what forces existed within a branch's system – the myriad of factors that caused inherent variances in performance – goals were created just as they are today: Using the dartboard method.

Nervous salespeople, desperately trying to achieve the 8% increase in spite of their system's unique factors that prevented it, scurried about securing high-risk business that was normally off limits, freight prone to damage and customers who required deep, unauthorized discounts and subsequent collection efforts. Additionally, salespeople felt like they had to make promises that they knew their operations and service counterparts could not keep, all in the name of making the almighty quota and thereby protecting their jobs.

Internal costs skyrocketed – paying loss and damage claims were a constant sore spot for the firm then – and the customer churn was high. The only good news was that our competitors promoted the same kind of destructive circus, so at least we were in good company with other P.T. Barnum's. However, the resulting race to the bottom would eventually collapse the entire industry.

In August of 1991, I returned to the field to helm a much larger branch, a beautiful facility in Manassas, Virginia. Located a stone's throw south from our nation's capital, I could not wait to take my new Deming-based philosophy out for a test drive. The branch had not shown a profit for some time – it was losing a nickel on every dollar when I arrived – so the task at hand was formidable. We were highly imbalanced, meaning that 70% of our freight was of the inbound variety, to be delivered locally, with only 30% heading outbound to other markets. That meant we were sending many empty trailers back out at night, a major profit killer.

As luck would have it, there was a major morning snowstorm that first winter season. Scores of over-the-road drivers, city drivers and dock personnel were stranded at the terminal with nothing but time on their hands. I had worked hard to position myself as a more employee-centric leader than they had been accustomed, so it was time to assess my efforts.

I walked into the break room with approximately 30 teamsters staring me down. Armed with six months worth of branch P&L statements, I handed out copies to everyone. "If we're getting paid, then we're going to work," I announced. This was the first time any real "management" information had ever touched their hands, and they looked at one another like their new manager had just escaped from a Stephen King novel. A low buzz ensued, and I broke it up by saying, "Today you officially become my business partners. May we start?"

The union steward, to my surprise, briefly scanned his flock, slowly stood and said, "You bet, boss." He then nodded to his constituency, signaling approval, and sat down. I could be wrong, but the man appeared a bit teary-eyed.

The next two hours were some of the most rewarding of my young career. As the fluffy white stuff filled the sky and ground, these gruff, grimy, hard-working men who had families and balanced their respective checkbooks weekly – also handling and hauling millions of dollars of freight each day – were finally treated as smart and responsible equals.

They learned how the branch made a profit, or did not, and asked enough intelligent questions to make my head spin.

Two specific examples resonate to this day. One man with three day-old scruff raised his hand and said, "We pay $3,000 a month for *electricity*? That's (expletive) crazy! Do you know that the shop (where maintenance is performed on company equipment) isn't even in use from midnight until around 6:00 AM, yet the lights burn all the while?"

I replied, "Didn't have a clue, Mick. And that's my fault." I thanked him and informed the group that we would remedy that situation immediately. Then I posed an important question to my new partners. "Why do we have the highest amount of returned deliveries in the region – maybe the entire company?"

The place sounded like a high school gym two hours after the dance. They just stared at each other, like the cat that had eaten the canary. I thought, *Wow, fear even rears its ugly head amongst teamsters.* Finally, the steward broke the silence. "Boss, the fact is that the load codes printed on shipment paperwork needs adjusting. You know, where it tells us to load the freight inside each trailer, so it's easy for the drivers to deliver on their routes?"

Before I could reply, all hell broke loose. City drivers began pointing fingers at the night dock men who loaded their city routes. "Charlie keeps loading my north deliveries on the rear, so I have to keep moving them around to get to my first deliveries. What's up with that, Charlie? Huh? Tell me, man!" This driver was the size of basketball's Shaquille O'Neal. And that's the way it went for five solid minutes. There was as much chewing tobacco airborne as there was snow descending from the heavens. I looked down upon what I had created, all of the open communication – toxic as it was – and was pleased beyond description.

"Whoa, fellas!" I finally yelled. "While I appreciate the spirited discussion, let me see if I've got this straight. Since the drivers rarely, if ever, see the guys who load their trailers at night, there's no feedback? No communication whatsoever between the two groups?"

"You got it, Sherlock!" Shaq said, cracking his neck.

The epiphany arrived. "And that's why all this stuff comes back every day?"

Shaq looked at me like I was an idiot. "Of course. And then the dock men re-handle it at night, jostling it around, unloading it and loading it all over again. Talk about doing the same job three and four times! Wanna save some money, boss? Then let's find out how each driver *wants* his truck loaded – screw those load codes – for maximum efficiency, and we'll get it loaded the right way. And, in case you ain't figured it out yet, that's why our loss and damage expense is so high, too. 'Cause we keep messing with the same freight when we should only have to touch it once!"

Humbled and head lowered, I didn't know what to say. Finally, the words came. "I'm very sorry, guys. You have my apologies. I didn't mean to make your working lives so miserable. I had no idea." The steward surveyed his minions, then said, "It's all good. Since you're the first manager to ever ask us our opinion, we'll help you out."

Within 60 days the electric bill was halved, and returned deliveries were reduced to 4% from 9%, saving hundreds of thousands of dollars in labor – the waste and rework type. Drivers became friendly with dock men, and the whole place perked up noticeably. Customers were thrilled with our new and improved level of service, and the P&L was taken off life support. We even garnered some positive attention from corporate headquarters in Overland Park, Kansas.

As I had anticipated, once word reached the regional office about what I had done, my crusty regional manager gave me an old-fashioned talking to about sharing sensitive information with "the help." And they wondered why their region had floundered for so long.

In the end, did our snow day "love-in" make things perfect? Absolutely not. Remember, teamsters are just about as screwed up as management, so some lines were never crossed, and progress keeps its own agenda. Still, we made headway that year and found common ground. Our conversations were never the same, but they were markedly *better*. Many of the men even asked astute questions about the statistical control charts we had posted, and the check sheets they were asked to complete. Collecting and analyzing data became commonplace, as did our joint discussions about root causes and proposed solutions.

It took 12 months, but to everyone's amazement, we turned a tidy profit in 1992.

Vilified, Ignored and Forgotten

How can this business genius (Deming), a primary catalyst in one of history's greatest economic achievements, be a relative unknown to most American business leaders at a time when they need him most? How have Dr. Deming's concepts become footnotes inside our schools and businesses while he is revered in Japan as a national savior and icon?

Here are five causes that must be fixed for American PRG improvement to occur:

1. **Unknown to the revenue side of the P&L.** Those traditionally responsible for designing value propositions, marketing campaigns and sales initiatives have not been exposed to Deming because his teachings are usually found on the manufacturing or operations side of the business.

2. **Top Management Accountability.** There is nothing that makes a top dog more uncomfortable than being cornered with all fingers pointed directly at her. Top management designed and created the systems and processes that employees work within, therefore it is *their* responsibility to enable infrastructure improvement. Far beyond the development of mission and vision statements, strategy and associated goals and objectives, continuous process improvement is the only activity that will improve quality, decrease costs and enhance customer demand. Anyone below top management is powerless to make these improvements without leadership's approval, commitment and ongoing ardent support.

3. **Short-term Thinking.** As long as the quarterly performance report remains paramount, intended to satisfy investors and stockholders, then more effective long-term thinking methodologies that help produce elite marketplace positioning don't stand a chance. Leadership has a primary responsibility to the future, to protect and provide jobs, and to ensure not only survival of the business, but the source code necessary for it to thrive. Unfortunately, too many senior leaders choose to protect their personal interests at the expense of the primary responsibility.

4. **Autocratic Reign.** For decades, many business leaders emerged from the military and sports arenas, dictatorial environments where management by fear, the proliferation of numerical goals and blind submission and loyalty are not only expected, but required. What worked for leadership drawn from those two bastions prior to 1990 no longer have a place today where people demand a higher sense of personal and corporate purpose, and satisfaction in their work, not to mention a strong amount of freedom to display their talents.

5. **Ignorance.** Many who are aware of Dr. Deming, either through formal education or otherwise, dismiss him as esoteric, even mystical. This happens for two reasons. First, they have not devoted the proper amount of time to fully comprehend and appreciate the master's tools and concepts. Second, Deming's philosophy is unconventional, flying directly in the face of many an MBA education. Management's belief systems, often protected by ego, arrogance and the fear to "fight city hall," are not easily changed, even when proof is evident. It is easy to dismiss that which does not easily fit into a paradigm when there is no one allowed to challenge.

NOTE: Deming's famed "14 Points for Management" – with a Revenution spin – is included in Appendix "A" at the end of this book.

Chapter 4

Surrogate:

The Only Reason the Sales Organization Exists (and it's not good)

"If your product requires advertising or salespeople to sell it, then it's not good enough"

~ Peter Thiel, Paypal co-founder; author of *Zero To One*

"The key to sustainable PRG in the third millennium is not 'selling,' it's designing, developing and delivering unprecedented value"

~ Sean Stormes

Completing the sentence: The only reason the Sales organization exists ... *is because demand does not.*

Most reasonable people would accept that statement as fact, if for no other reason than sheer logic. After all, why would salespeople be necessary if customers bought simply because "they had to have it?" Therefore, leadership's primary objective is to intentionally and purposefully design, develop and deliver substantial customer demand.

This singular concept is the PRG game-changer. Substitute the word "marketing" for "sales" and the statement would still be accurate. For example, have you seen ads for Tesla or Five Guys Burgers and Fries? Of course not! How about the existence of traditional salespeople at the Apple store, or are there just friendly, knowledgeable facilitators who help accomplish whatever task is at hand? In each case, loyal customers patronize these businesses because strong demand delivers them there.

I led sales organizations large, medium and small from 1984 through 2008, including stints at two Fortune 500 firms, two mid-market and two small businesses. I devoured the sales gurus' respective books, tapes and columns with varying degrees of success. But it wasn't until I was introduced to the concepts (source code) of demand creation and "attraction" that my PRG worldview changed. At the core of my transformation was finally submitting to what I knew to be true regarding the sales profession.

To witness, a telling 2015 (February 6) Wall Street Journal article by Lauren Weber stated, "Some companies are having a hard time selling people on a career in sales." Why? Ms. Weber reported the following:

- Employers say young workers are uninterested in sales, a field they perceive as risky and defined by competition.

- Employers spent an average of 41 days trying to fill sales jobs, compared with an average of 33 days for all jobs for the 12-month period ending in September 2014, according to Burning Glass, a labor-market analysis firm that worked with Harvard Business School on the report.

- Paycor Inc., which sells cloud-based software for human-resources and payroll management, said it would have forecast $2 million more in 2015 revenue if it had hit its 2014 hiring goals for new sales reps in 2014.

- The youngest generation of workers, having lived through the financial crisis and recession, is more risk-averse, say sales executives, adding that young prospects are reluctant to enter a hard-charging work environment where success often boils down to a number.

- "There is a huge stereotype that sales is not really a career—that either anyone can do it or you're born to it," said Suzanne Fogel, chair of the marketing department at DePaul University's Driehaus College of Business. Parents share some of those misconceptions, and often dissuade their children from pursuing sales careers, she added.

- As companies become savvier about the products they buy, wheeler-dealers are out, and problem-solvers are in.

- "If you asked me six months ago if I'd become a salesman, I would've said absolutely not," said Tom Keenan, then a 21 year-old senior at Bryant University in Rhode Island, noting that he had assumed that "salespeople only sold products to take the consumers' money—and that bothered me."

Broken, Ineffective Source Code

If there is one group of people who will validate what you are about to read on this journey, it is your customers. They have just about had it with salespeople. But why?

Many who gravitate toward the sales profession are talkers, having been told for a lifetime that they were "natural born salespeople," always prepared to pitch ice to anyone they perceive as an Eskimo. True to form, logic never occurs to these people: *Eskimos don't need ice.* Worse, this damaging feedback becomes a never-ending self-affirmation. The embodiment of "Life of The Party," their ears rarely work.

They meet the standard salesperson profile according to the multiple personality tests completed: money-motivated; persistent; hard worker (sometimes); sociable. Their respective sales performance during the boom years was as impressive as any.

Additionally, the sales training each received from three nationally known firms provided a formal sales process blueprint to follow, and "proven" techniques for virtually any selling scenario. They are convinced that making it big in sales is all about *them* – their drive, their knowledge, their skills, their charming personality. In fact, that is what their bosses have preached to them since the day they were hired.

The pressure to drive sales is enormous due to the system his company's leadership designed. Why else employ salespeople, if not to drive revenue? The Marketing department develops positioning and consumer interest – setting up metaphorical pins – and Sales knocks 'em down! It's been that way since the Dead Sea was merely sick.

Of course, our traditional salesperson (and the organization's leadership) believe that they have exactly what customers want, and that it is just a matter of making these hungry buyers aware of the wonderful benefits they provide. Salespeople then cold call, smiling and dialing, interrupting and generally wasting a lot of time on low-ROI activities, unknowingly upsetting a potentially lucrative prospect base along the way. They have trouble getting appointments, having calls returned and gaining commitments.

And the leadership team still cannot pinpoint the root cause of stagnant sales performance.

The Revenution: Part II

Any excuses for not capturing an abundance of profitable revenue – the lifeblood of every enterprise – have been vanquished, as in trampled, crushed and buried for eternity. Regardless of category, product or service, elite revenue performance is yours for the taking. What are you waiting for? There is a revenue revolution occurring, a complete overthrow of the old guard that is transforming the way entire industries attract and delight passionate, devoted customers. Are you aware of this global rebellion, and the people, companies and specific architecture behind its ascent?

The traditional sales and marketing "Which is more integral to improved revenue?" debate is moot. The only issue of consequence is whether or not a group of like-minded people clamors for you and your stuff. The rest is an easy button. No clamor? No attraction? No demand? Then the possibility for (organic) PRG is nil. However, status quo thinking on this critical matter has been replaced by intentional, counterintuitive and elegant design. Simple in concept, some have said, though difficult in execution. If it were easy, we would all be swimming in greenbacks, right?

The Revenution

Critical, select components of the PRG ecosystem, identified and aligned, that result in a business development process used by progressive industry leaders to dominate their respective categories.

Building our case for the Revenution demands a long overdue analysis and debunking of the sales profession's age old "best practices," the core of what many in the vocation hold near and dear to their hearts. While most senior executives see their respective "value proposition bowls" teeming with significance, worth and hope, which turns into confusion and frustration when sales forecasts are left unfulfilled, the reality is grim, though most refuse to accept the reality.

Similar to the hit movie *The Matrix*, there are forces that have led us to believe and trust in a world – a growth model, in this case – that simply does not exist, bolstered by a unique set of forces and circumstances providing a false sense of comfort. The century-old sales game ruse is about to be exposed.

Take the red pill, Neo, and prepare to enter the real world.

Illusion #1: Salesperson Value In The Third Millennium

Have you ever questioned why the concept of salespeople, as the supposed true drivers of company revenue, endures decade after decade displaying the resiliency of cockroaches? Please think about this with an open mind: What causes the salesperson's very existence? Are they really necessary, especially with the technology consumers now have at their fingertips? What exactly is the salesperson's role? What are they really selling? *What high value do they actually provide?*

Noodle on that for a moment while we ponder other important questions.

Salespeople have been performing their jobs the same way since the first bottle of snake oil was pitched, farming and hunting, then farming and hunting some more. Outbound prospecting, cold calling, persuading, convincing, cajoling and manipulating have long been the salesperson's wretched life. Customers despise the approach, and many salespeople dislike it even more. It is just not a natural behavior, and studies continue to validate these emotions. How then does this archaic practice survive?

Do departments including Finance, Human Resources, Engineering, Administration, Information Technology and Marketing perform their important jobs the same way they did 100 years ago, not to mention just ten years ago? Each has evolved, no longer dragging its respective knuckles along the business highway. Why then has the sales vocation not progressed, advancing as others have?

Consider the customer referral system industry. It is growing rapidly, teaching salespeople the supposed hidden secrets to extracting valuable recommendations. Ask yourself, why exactly do salespeople need formal systems to get happy clients to refer them? Why do they have to ask for referrals in the first place? Why don't customers feel compelled to make recommendations without the manipulative prompting and begging from a salesperson? Could it be that current customer experiences are unworthy of risking the most important asset they possess – their reputation? If that is true, what does that say about the salesperson, and more importantly, their company's value proposition?

Additionally, most business owners and top executives believe their salespeople are in the occupation of "Business Development." This perception is often the furthest thing from truth.

In the early 2000s, global industrial supply giant Grainger, Inc. commissioned an internal study to determine how much time salespeople actually spent in front of customers. Top management was dismayed to learn that salespeople were face to face with customers only 25% of the time. Much of the non-customer face time was driven by corporate directives – meetings and reporting requirements being the top two culprits – though Grainger leadership would not admit to that fact. Still, salespeople can be their own worst enemies, exacerbated by clueless sales managers who are generally overworked and woefully unqualified for their jobs.

Other than meetings and reporting requirements, it is a surprise to many outside the sales profession to learn what salespeople do with their day. The majority of salespeople are what I've coined "One-Through-Four's." They perform four primary duties, none of which actually develops business:

1. **Order Taker.** Obvious? Like orders cannot be electronically submitted to the office? Most salespeople love milling around, "in the name of the customer," appearing busy, especially under the guise of "Just making another sale, boss!" Rule #1: Never mistake activity for results.

2. **Technician.** Salespeople receive more product knowledge education than any other form of training in their careers. No wonder they can't help but show off their alleged prowess once in front of customers, especially since most are of the loquacious variety. If you received 200 hours of product knowledge annually, wouldn't you be dying to share with others, too? The Technician-wearing-salesperson's-clothing often performs some version of the following functions that should be left to others: Designer; project manager; measurer; information provider; craftsman.

3. **Firefighter.** Ah, the "problem solver." The white knight that revels in mitigating disaster at the 11th hour by navigating their company's internal labyrinth. These glory hounds relish train wrecks. It provides them the opportunity to right great wrongs, claiming praise from thankful customers who make sure the salesperson's superiors know that they had better never dismiss their knight, or risk losing business. The Firefighter complains about the ineptness of his company's proficiency, yet secretly craves just one more chance to shine – to save the day. He rarely offers solutions to root causes of recurring problems, of course. After all, why eliminate the source of his job security?

4. **Customer Service Agent.** Talk about the mother of all time bandits. Here are just a few activities performed by salespeople, individuals more suited to old-fashioned account management: Collecting money; fixing invoice errors; answering mundane questions; providing samples; making deliveries; answering the phone; handling miscellaneous administrative tasks.

The traditional salesperson's place in the business universe is becoming extinct as technology, and common sense, evolves.

At some companies, including Wal-Mart, decision-makers refuse to see salespeople. Prospective vendors provide information electronically, and Wal-Mart employees perform their due diligence without ever seeing a One-Through-Four.

They have designed a more efficient purchasing process, and if you think Wal-Mart flourishes with this tactic because they are merely a low price provider, uninterested in discussing value, guess again. The concept is garnering interest within other industries, primarily because the cost savings realized by not wasting time with value-less salespeople is colossal.

There's no place for One-Through-Fours in the Revenution.

Illusion #2: The Sales Training Industry

What if you attended an acclaimed engineering school, educated by elite, accomplished professors? Then, to your surprise – *post-graduation* – remote and unfamiliar gurus climbed from the muck proclaiming a plethora of new methods regarding how engineering should be performed.

Would you buy into the hype? Consider, as of this writing, that there are approximately only 100 U.S. colleges and universities currently offering a major or minor in formal sales education. That dearth of accredited programs creates a huge opportunity for anyone who claims credibility to capitalize on. Quoting the Michael Douglas movie *An American President*: "In the absence of genuine leadership, (people will) listen to anyone who steps up to the microphone. They're so thirsty for it, they'll crawl through the desert to a mirage, and when they discover there is no water, they will drink the sand."

And that is how we end up with The Usual Suspects.

> **Fact:** 86% of salespeople do not achieve 90% of their annual quota. In other words, only 14% succeed, or 1.4 out of 10.[3]
>
> **Fact:** $15 billion is spent annually on sales training in the United States.[4]

That math does not work, or as my good friends from the South might say, "That dog won't hunt." It never has. Pathetic ROI is exactly that – *pathetic*.

Over the years, management and salespeople have been seduced by popular sales gurus and their impressive marketing machines, keeping them top of mind in a profession that churns out new prospects (salespeople) by the *second*. It is a lucrative business in spite of a severely flawed premise, primarily because of no apparent alternatives. Additionally, most testimonials attributed to the benefits of sales training are almost always propagated by a small percentage that succeed

---

[3] 2008 Miller Heiman study

[4] 2009 *Sales and Marketing* magazine

despite the training (and because of other important factors that we will review), and swindled executives who are too embarrassed and ashamed to admit the truth. More than a few senior leaders have shared this with me long after the shame faded.

To be clear, the very nature of sales training makes two incorrect assumptions:

1. The salesperson's company possesses value that customers deeply desire.
2. Sales occur most often because of the salesperson's efforts.

The sales trainer's focus is on the salesperson *making a sale*, a self-serving activity if there ever was one. This does not bode well for long-term success. The salesperson is not the purchasing linchpin, as we will learn. He is a garnish, at best. However, if he *is* the linchpin, his company is exposed and unprotected. If customers buy because of their salesperson, what does that say about the company's value proposition? The reasons why customers buy should correlate directly to a company's (unprecedented) value proposition – not its salespeople.

For years, The Usual Suspects have had you right where they wanted, but no longer. Would you rather hand over your One-Through-Four salespeople – with an objective of sustainable PRG – to someone who bought a sales training franchise with the purpose of lining *their* pockets, or create real, sustainable customer demand that does not depend on One-Through-Fours?

If we lump in The Usual Suspects from bygone eras – name your wealthy sales guru – I believe we end up with a dangerous elixir. Traditional, hokey salesmanship is a dinosaur, dusty bones entombed far below the earth's surface.

It is time to evolve and follow progressive industry leaders to a more effective PRG model.

Illusion #3: Ignoring the Deadliest Business Disease

Year after year, discussions with company executives follow a pattern that provides keen insight into their PRG woes, inevitably pointing to a dominant culprit. The most destructive business disease on the planet that has reached epidemic proportions is *sameness*. This omnipresent virus initially manifests itself as vulnerability, a masked condition that most senior level managers are oblivious to because of runaway ego (like Tony the Tiger: *Weeee're Great!*) and lack of meaningful customer connectivity (what, no spreadsheet for emotional perceptions?).

Subsequently, sameness evolves into the lethal station known as *irrelevance*. Similar to an unanticipated electric shock, executives only seem to emerge from their sameness funk when top line revenue tanks, though by then they are experiencing a free fall to the point of no return. The damage results in a marketplace perception abyss that is most often difficult to recover from.

Many marketers fall into the same trap. Third party marketing firms often use a client's sameness offering as raw material when developing and amplifying brand messaging and promises to the masses ("strengths" and "differentiation" are most often mirages). Fanning the flames of sameness does nothing but expose a company's insignificance to a marketplace that seeks its true north.

While evolution – often referred to as the copycat economy – is a primary component of sameness, it is more important to comprehend that most products and services are viewed as commodities. That's not supposition. Prove it to yourself by making a list of all competitors. Is there more than just you in the marketplace? Do your competitors provide similar products and services? If yes, then there is a strong possibility that sameness is beating a path to your doorstep, if it is not already knocking hard.

Therefore, what should you really be offering? What is it that ultimately attracts your ideal, coveted "dream clients?" How do you strike the genuine customer chord?

Illusion #4: The Invisible Value Proposition

What is it about your company that allows it to boldly stand out and attract dream clients? What constitutes real competitive advantage? Here are the 15 answers that top management, and their charges, proclaim most often during my presentations, workshops and consulting projects:

Culture	Technology	People
Knowledge	Brand	Education
Tenure Skill	Service	Reputation
Product Selection	Location(s)	Training

Professionalism   Product performance

Yawn. Pass the smelling salts, please.

How do any of those over-used, generic words matter to the *customer*? How are they interpreted, and which ones resonate deeply, creating a strong connection? Which of these attributes might tip the buying decision in one's favor? During economic downturns, customers become more discerning as technology continues its meteoric proliferation and utility. Companies slash costs to the bone to eke out a profit, unintentionally resulting in reduced service, while marketplace white noise soars to deafening levels. With these dynamic forces in play, the above-listed competitive advantages are revealed as anything but.

Companies become exposed as providing little or no value, however senior leadership remains staunch believers that their value proposition glass is full to the brim. Just ask them. To the contrary, the glass is often perceived by prospects as near empty, and that makes this issue a primary opportunity for PRG improvement. The disparity that exists between what top management assumes and what their customers require not only correlates directly to important metrics including margins and sales conversion ratios, but to company survival as well.

One study, focused on mid-market companies, found that only two CEOs out of 1,000 who were asked to clearly and accurately articulate their competitive advantages could do so. The other 99.8% could offer only vague, imprecise generalities.[5] This is how companies end up missing the genuine customer chord "bulls-eye" and embracing ineffective, me-too value propositions. The CEO, most often, has the final say regarding company direction, specifically in the areas of marketing, branding and sales. The CEOs perception is so dominant that it often overrules the Chief Marketing Officer's recommendations.

To make matters worse, the vast majority of marketers are not versed in the Revenution philosophy. Consider that the previous list of 15 is usually the raw material – *the actual ingredients* – used in the creation of a company's sales and marketing collateral. Websites, business cards, advertising, sales pitches, slide decks and more employ sameness as a primary reason for doing business with the company. This is the almighty value proposition, used to convince prospects to leave their current providers and give you a shot? This is what

---

[5] *Creating Competitive Advantage*, by Jaynie L. Smith with William G. Flanagan

the CEO wants you to go to war with – arrows with dull, rubber tips? How do you feel about that?

Perform the following exercise:

Review ten competitors' websites, then click through to the "Why Choose Us/How We're Different" tab. Compare your findings to the previous list of 15, then take two aspirin and call me in the morning.

Leadership's Fatal Presumptions

Now that we have exposed the sales profession for what it really is – One-Through-Fours; The Usual Suspects; the Deadliest Business Disease; and The Invisible Value Proposition – you are primed for the Nine Fatal Leadership Presumptions.

The following list is a gift carefully and specifically assembled just for you, a mighty compass to wield when shattering archaic and destructive paradigms – the primary obstacles to PRG improvement. When breaking free from urban legend, expert weaponry is required to fend off those who grip the familiar and comfortable, are blinded from the truth, and fear change more than death and taxes.

Belief systems are forged by three factors: attitudes, experiences and success. Therefore, when anything appears counter to those factors, i.e. anything new, then sticky paradigms launch their internal defense, battening down the hatches, securing the fort from interlopers. It is a natural reaction, and that is where the PRG battle is lost because it is the "unnatural" – the counterintuitive – that wins in the Revenution.

Paradigms guide thinking and attitudes, which subsequently drive actions and behaviors. Actions and behaviors drive results. To experience different results, affect the paradigm. That is why the Revenution is a formal design process versus a downloaded template based on what seems intuitive. We must move from "intuitive to intentional."

There are reasons why so many companies have not yet reached PRG success and sustainability. Their belief systems must be adequately addressed before exploring potential solutions. To be great, one must study greatness. And, as Revenution converts tell me, those with responsibility for sales should first be de-programmed, their sticky paradigm "glass" emptied before they can even consider an alternative.

Without further adieu:

Nine Fatal Leadership Presumptions

1. The company's value proposition is just and drives ample customer demand
2. Company departments operate in synergy, creating a formidable value chain
3. Company leadership understands, and owns, its brand
4. PRG is a sales organization responsibility (and no one else's)
5. Marketing creates interest and demand, while salespeople drive revenue
6. Sales training is a proven, high-ROI activity and investment
7. Customers need salespeople to make purchasing decisions

8. Both good and bad PRG performance is caused by the same set of factors
9. Reviewing historical data aids in predicting future outcomes

We will refer back to these presumptions often, but for now, please know that leadership's perception of how PRG occurs is skewed, and that is why their companies struggle to grow. They have been told by adoring (and fearful) peers, subordinates and consultants for years that their new suits are amazing, the best in all the land! Unfortunately, it is all one big illusion.

In reality, the emperor has no clothes.

Section II

The Intentional Design of Organizational Fitness

Chapter 5

Steam:

Engineering the
Unbeatable Advantage

"Organizational health will surpass all other disciplines in business as the greatest opportunity for improvement and competitive advantage"

~ Patrick Lencioni, Author

"It is senior leadership's charge to build a human-based, impenetrable moat around their economic castle that competitors cannot cross"

~ Sean Stormes

There are seven billion people on the planet, yet none of them share the same fingerprints. Engineering exclusivity – becoming known as "the only ones who do what you do" – should be your goal in the ongoing battle against sameness and the search for sustainable PRG.

Most everything in business can be copied, including products, services, strategies, websites, processes, awards, traditional branding, and even leadership as executives hop from company to company. The only element that *cannot* be copied is a specific group of people, their (unflinching) belief system, and how those beliefs manifest into daily behaviors and actions, all driven by carefully crafted processes that produce the desired end result. This is how absolute commitment is forged, baked into everything and anything to ensure that the belief system becomes operationalized. Otherwise, it is just another set of motivational-sounding words residing on laminated cards, tucked deep into a forgotten drawer.

Comprehensive organizational alignment – the exclusive fingerprint – is a foolproof way that company stakeholders can experience much-needed clarity, particularly regarding purpose, direction and an understanding of why and how to do their respective jobs.

When organizational alignment and clarity are achieved, the following key attributes blossom:

- **Speed.** Less ambiguity and confusion paves the way for increased efficiency. Shared ideology has a habit of accomplishing that. For example, the number of meetings can be drastically reduced, improving productivity.

- **Inspiration.** Employees who overachieve tend to be inspired vs. "motivated" or incented. And when companies strike the genuine customer chord, people tend to remain loyal through crises.

- **Culture.** Culture is a result, not a program or strategy. It is the natural residue of the degree of alignment and clarity that exists between people. What do most of them, if not all, have in common? What shared attributes drive the company forward?

- **Customer Experience.** The more value customers perceive, the more they spend – often paying a premium – therefore *how* they interact with a company is paramount. Is your customer experience – the specific peak moments therein – intentionally and purposefully designed, touch point by touch point, to yield something compelling, memorable and remarkable? How is it measured, and are those metrics "Job One" on leadership's dashboard?

- **Attraction: Part I.** When executed at a high level, the "right fit" people will clamor to work for your company. Organizational Fitness resists loading up the enterprise purely with the "smartest" people. Rather, purpose-drive leaders seek the right fit, too. For proof, put 10 of the smartest people you can find in a room and ask them to solve a problem while reaching consensus. Say it with me now: G-R-I-D-L-O-C-K.

- **Attraction: Part II.** Alignment and clarity also helps establish positioning that attracts similar, purpose-driven prospects – dream clients. What a company *stands for* is far more important than what it *sells*. What do you want to be known for that can hasten the realization of the coveted Attractor status?

Misaligned, unclear or incompetent leadership causes virtually all company dysfunction and poor performance. They are the sole designers of all company systems and process, i.e. how the work gets done.

Chapter 6

Truancy:

The Missing Ingredient That Dooms Most PRG Efforts

"Absence makes the heart grow fonder"

~ Author Unknown

"If the heart – the organization – grows fonder for its absent leader, then the resulting void creates irreparable damage"

~ Sean Stormes

There is a reason why many of Dr. Deming's 14 Points imply or directly invoke the word "leadership" versus mere management. Without what author Jim Collins referred to in his seminal book, *Good to Great*, as "Level Five Leadership," PRG struggles indefinitely to reach its full potential.

Level Five leadership is not only humble and willful, Collins explains, it also involves being "present," something we will get to in a moment. Every CEO or business owner I have had the pleasure of working with who successfully executed The Third Door architecture – and realized jaw-dropping PRG – possessed high levels of humility and willfulness. And, to a person, those who were narcissists, arrogant, greedy or entitled (that's a big one) failed miserably, doomed to a life of sameness, high waste and rework costs, roller coaster quarterly and annual performance, and overall marketplace mediocrity.

Further explanation of Collins' two key senior leadership traits:

- **Humble.** They believe in servant leadership, there to help everyone in the organization win, up to and including exhibiting "compassionate leadership," i.e. exiting low performers out of the organization so the employee can be successful elsewhere. Additionally, humble leaders are comfortable in knowing that they do not have to possess the best ideas, gladly giving credit where it is due. They see their job as clearing obstacles, providing resources, living the company purpose, and steering the ship, all in the name of *others*. In Under Armour's vernacular, senior leadership is there to "Protect This House," and everyone who resides under its collective roof.

- **Willful.** When leaders are "resolute" – driven to succeed – and combine that attribute with inherent, sincere humility, they become vastly more effective than those who do not possess these genuine qualities.

Which brings us to "being present." It still mystifies me that this even needs explaining, since every successful business owner or CEO that I have ever met works as hard, or harder, than just about anyone at their respective company. They show up before anyone else, leave late, are demanding relative to holding their direct reports accountable for the specific processes that drive results, know the numbers backwards and forwards, are respectful, and practically will the organization to new heights on a regular basis. They are not easily influenced, possess an enviable network of outside-their-industry mentors to regularly learn from, and recognize that while "purpose before profit" sounds noble, it is *profit dollars* that allow the purpose to be fulfilled. Accountability is more than a watchword – it also comes with clearly communicated consequences.

Leaders that are present rarely "check out," because if they do they realize that entitlement will be the residue that others sense quickly. "Hey, if the boss isn't here – or obviously isn't engaged in the business – then why should we bust our ass?" Don't laugh as I have heard those actual words more times than I would like to admit. Another axiom I have heard many times is, "Ownership has its privileges." That's fine. But to be clear, those "privileges" should never include being absent on a regular basis.

Five Primary Reasons For Absent (Real) Leadership

- **Pedigree.** Whether it is higher education, social status or resume, a select few rise to power because of upper crust, blue blood lineage. Entitlement sometimes trumps competency and qualification. Just because someone has money does not mean they should be in charge of people – and the livelihoods of those people's families.

- **Command and Control.** You know these people as monomaniacal, pompous and egocentric. Think "bully." They are proud of and thrive on the rampant organizational fear they have intentionally established and rule over.

- **Inheritance.** Family-owned businesses face unique challenges, however the ones that go awry often allow blatant favoritism and protectionism. A dictatorial and tyrannical leadership ethos creates deafening, company-wide silence, resulting in horrible workplaces and substandard organizational performance. Still, as long as the family "gets theirs," everyone else can be damned. #Selfish

- **Spreadsheet jockeys.** Numbers, numbers, *NUMBERS!* These bean counters avoid customers like the plague, a convenient shield from accountability and truth. With low empathy (emotional intelligence), curiosity and adaptability quotients, they embody the ancient exhortation "Open Door Policy," never realizing that no one ever enters this type of leader's door. Truth be told, employees avoid it like the plague. These leaders also eschew customer research, once again fearful of the truth. Never able to embrace "the uncomfortable," they live in a safe bubble that eventually destroys the company.

- **Professional Incest.** Occasionally present when investors are involved, "keeping things in the (business) family" supersedes the needs of the organization. When actual investors become part of a company leadership team, the sole focus is on profits – a most dangerous proposition because profitability is merely a result. What *drives* profitability in the third millennium is much more important and crucial to repeatable, sustainable success. Yet those third millennium success drivers (the PRG recipe contained within this book) are foreign to the vast majority of status quo leadership.

The "present leader" finds absenteeism – *truancy* – offensive, and will often avoid these types of "hide and seek" owners. The present leader knows that like it or not, the success of the business is primarily due to their attendance, beliefs, obsessions, requirements, demands, communication, knowledge and overall involvement. They see their stake as the key ingredient to success or failure of the enterprise. Therefore, delegating this stake to others – trading deep involvement for entitled absenteeism – is considered not only not acceptable, but a death knell.

Show me a failing organization, and I will show you an often-absent head honcho.

Chapter 7

Linchpin:

Got Purpose? (Part I)

"Whatsoever a man soweth, that shall he also reap"

~ From the Bible, Galatians VI (King James Version)

"Sooner or later, a rudderless boat will find rocky shores"

~ Sean Stormes

Some senior executives, after hearing one of my keynote speeches, become excited by the thought of un-evening their respective competitive playing fields. Visions of runaway PRG and 5X company valuations dance in their heads.

Approaching, each "thinks" they want to reimagine, reinvent and ultimately transform their business model – and in the process, the company. Unfortunately reality does not match perception. As proof, read what most CEOs and business owners said when asked *why* they are in business:

"To sell products and services to our industry"

"We strive to be the best in everything we do"

"To make money"

As you can see, those types of statements, erroneously referred to as "mission statements" by many, are not only unable to provide organizational true north – providing acute alignment and clarity – there is no teeth, no inspiration, no aspirational cause to strive for. They are not even remotely in the same zip code of how the company is trying to make a difference in people's lives.

Exacerbating the problem, when senior leadership teams live under separate beliefs as to why the company exists, a plethora of destructive erosion can occur, including organizational A.D.D., silos and divisiveness among the ranks. As dissension and uncertainty take root, costly waste and rework multiplies as profitability plummets. And since waste and rework can amount to as much as 25% to 40% of annual top line revenue (really think about that for a moment), the financial hit can be substantial.

The business component that consistently scales faster than any other is *meaning*. The following diagram by author, cartoonist and pundit Hugh MacLeod of gapingvoid fame may explain this concept best:

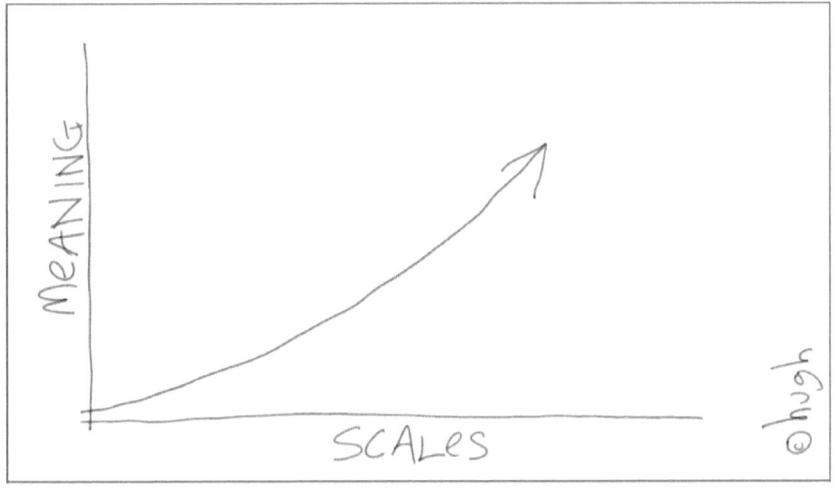

How meaningful is the company to its customers? In other words, how does the organization *matter* to the people it serves? To what degree does it show it cares, on a daily basis, helping people feel more like they want to feel, and achieve more of what they are trying to achieve? How does the organization's purpose reveal itself through the core characteristics of its products and services? Why should everyone join the movement? What is in it for them?

Simon Sinek's best-selling book, *Start With Why*, while excellent, does not delve deep enough into what true organizational purpose is, why it is critical for sustainable success, and how it is designed, developed and delivered. Similarly, Sinek's popular TED talk, highlighting the Golden Circle concept (also excellent), only discloses the 'why' behind which features will resonate with customers – independent of the core product or service.

We will go into greater depth regarding the design of company purpose in Chapter 11, *Got Purpose (Part II)*, but for now please understand that lack of purpose is one of the three primary causes of sameness, the business disease that's reached epidemic proportions. It is also a primary cause of substandard PRG. Virtually every company suffers from an identity crisis, and not knowing who they are – and who they are *not* – adversely affects the P&L and the firm's very survival. If one day the organization behaves as Dr. Jekyll, and the next day shows up as Mr. Hyde, then variation exists – and that variation correlates directly to higher costs, missed opportunities, employee disengagement and dissatisfaction, not to mention customer confusion and disillusionment of the brand.

Solving this toxic behavior should be one of senior leadership's primary tasks.

Chapter 8

"Do":

More Powerful Than Values

"He lived exclusively for his art and in sharp contrast to most painters of today who never lift a paintbrush to canvas without thought of the box office results ... he had the courage of his principles."

~ Henry McBride, Art Critic, on painter Alfred Henry Maurer

"If doubling revenue in the next 12-24 months is desired, then let people clearly and unequivocally know what you stand for"

~ Sean Stormes

My hunch is that you have seen more organizations prominently display their self-proclaimed values than those who do not. Another hunch is that at least occasionally, you have had a poor experience with such companies, prompting a comment similar to, "So much for their supposed 'values.'"

If actions truly speak louder than words, then consider behaviors as an effective alternative to all too often impotent values, i.e. supercharged actions wrapped in daily habits. It is those core habits – identified, shaped, measured and modeled by senior leadership that the organization is held accountable to – that separates authenticity from fraud. Remember, practice does not make perfect. Practice makes *permanent*. The question then becomes, "What are you and your organization making permanent each and every day?"

The distinction between values and behaviors is important to comprehend. For example, as we know, leaders should never mistake activity for results. If sustainable PRG is your objective, then identifying core, actionable behaviors that align with company purpose is critical to results. The greater the misalignment between core behaviors and purpose, the fuzzier, uncertain and more confused the organization becomes regarding what it stands for. Remember, as highlighted in Chapter Three, *Wise Old Sage & The Power of Harnessing Variation*, as systemic variation (misalignment) increases within the system (your organization), waste and rework also increases, driving significant hidden costs through the roof and destroying the P&L. This direct correlation cannot be denied.

As proof, here are just a few examples of costly waste and rework caused by misaligned core behaviors and purpose, or the total absence of organizational fitness:

- Flavor of the month strategies
- Entry into non-core or unprofitable markets
- Passive aggressive (or overt) infighting
- Confusion
- Project scope creep
- Poor decision-making
- Hiring Practices
- Solicitation or retention of profit-killing customers
- Silos

The most effective leaders excel in managing the *drivers* that fulfill the purpose. These drivers act as pistons for the purpose/PRG engine. Additionally, these enlightened leaders have learned that "the objective is not to grow, but rather to fulfill the purpose."

The Five Steps to Designing Powerful Core Behaviors

1. **Operational definition.** Think "virtue." Belief. Ideal. Ethic. Principle. Rule. Foundation. Organizational truth. Heavy stuff, right? How about this word: *Obsession*. These are key elements to the core behavior compass. It can take months for leadership teams to identify and agree upon these critical "purpose pistons." Similar to designing purpose, senior management will most often disagree on core behaviors, even if they have been working together for years. Frequently, their initial answers are not even in the same zip code. While this is an indictment on other organizational maladies, caused by the same leadership team, most often they are willing to explore for the sake of the enterprise – though occasionally an emotionally unintelligent senior leader will self-deselect and leave the company, citing, "I didn't sign up for this Kumbaya foolishness." Surprised? Don't be. This type of behavior tends to be the norm, particularly at the top of companies where the almighty dollar often rules actions and decisions to the detriment of creating sustainable, unprecedented value. The good news is that

once the team becomes mindful of the exercise, exhibiting requisite humility and vulnerability, the elusive beliefs and principles begin to emerge. As debate, editing and polishing ensues, the team finally unites, more aligned and clear than ever before. And the organization wins big.

2. **Core behaviors are not "minimum acceptable" behaviors.** Basic virtues, including work ethic, honesty, integrity, teamwork and the like, should be the floor for any organization, i.e. minimum standards for employment. Would you really hire someone that you knew was lazy, dishonest, corrupted, deceitful, argumentative and prone to go rogue to the detriment of others? Of course not! Conversely, what is the company's existing DNA – its heredity – that allows it to not just compete, but more importantly what customers and other stakeholders point to that is *unprecedented*, allowing the organization to create significant marketplace separation? In my practice, we have seen wonderful core behaviors like collaboration, curiosity and "run to the problem" excavated from the recesses of a company's labyrinth. Choosing core behaviors requires setting the highest of bars.

a. Which behaviors can you say you safely "own" vs. your competitors?
b. Can the leadership team unanimously and confidently agree, and prove, that the organization has a 98% higher mastery with the chosen behaviors vs. competitors?
c. Be certain that core behaviors are real – not a wish list. Still, identifying aspirational behaviors is also important so the organization continues to evolve, forever striving to fulfill the purpose.

Since there are strong expectations and accountability attached to core behaviors, please remember that what gets measured gets managed, and what gets managed gets done. How can you guarantee that core behaviors will be effectively lived? See #5 below, and Chapter 21, *Full Integration: Baking the New Model Into the Company's Bones*, for a more comprehensive explanation.

3. **Three is the magic number.** One or two behaviors are too few and ineffective – not enough pistons to drive the purpose engine – while more than three diminishes importance, strength and capability. Besides,

there is scientific proof that three main points resonate – holds more sustainable power – than any other number.

4. **Core behaviors are not etched in stone.** While the company's purpose statement is permanent, core behaviors often have a shelf life depending on the needs of the business.

5. **Ensuring success.** When leadership is committed to leveraging the power of purpose and core behaviors on organizational fitness and PRG, people are recognized, rewarded, disciplined, terminated and promoted in direct correlation to their visible alignment with the company's principles. As proof, well-known and respected leaders including Tony Hsieh of Zappos, John Mackey of Whole Foods Market and Southwest Air's Gary Kelly adhere to this ethos, providing keen insight into why those companies have been wildly successful for decades, each a dominant market leader.

An Important Note About Following Processes

While the word "process" is used liberally throughout this book, please do not confuse it with "rigid." An empowered team – one that has been thoroughly trained and given access to all necessary data and other information to succeed, allowing them to make the same quality of decision that management makes – must have the latitude to do what they believe is right. Process provides a guideline, a path. It is not intended to be the only way to do something, because nothing in life is static.

Take the well-documented United Airlines incident from April 2017, where a man was dragged from his seat and hit repeatedly when refusing to deplane after he was randomly selected. U.A. employees "followed process" to the letter, leaving in their wake a tidal wave of public ill will.

Moral of the story: Do not place an expectation for employees to blindly follow processes. Hopefully you did not hire people to act as robots. Rather, processes are merely guidelines, often helpful in the training phase. Especially when it comes to customer-related issues, people should be encouraged and trusted to use their best judgment.

Chapter 9

Wisdom:

Choosing the Most Effective Game Plan

"Perception is strong, and sight weak. In strategy it is important to see distant things as if they were close, and to take a distanced view of close things"

~ Miyamoto Musashi,
legendary Japanese
swordsman

"A primary cause of profit-killing waste and rework, apart from doing nothing, is choosing the wrong course of action"

~ Sean Stormes

Once an organization has found its purpose – the cause or movement people rally around – and associated core behavior "pistons," leadership must effectively execute or risk program-of-the-month syndrome, or worse, organizational apathy. Execute what, though? Choose the wrong path and both short and long-term performance suffers, up to and including extinction (see the Slippery Business Death Slope in Chapter 1). Choose the right path, and PRG nirvana is within reach.

Without senior leadership's firm commitment to organizational principles and subsequent strategies, including associated plans and objectives, scope creep and silo-building will most likely occur, resulting in expensive organizational

A.D.D. It can become "every person for themselves" as variation breeds, swelling at a rapid pace. If you have ever wondered why top line revenue can be healthy while profitability suffers, now you have the answer. The cost of uninspired or "flat" game planning – steering the enterprise without True North – has sabotaged many startups and former market-dominant companies.

If purpose is why the company exists and the difference it is trying to make in people's lives, then the mission statement is the *primary strategy* that fulfills the purpose. I am betting that you have seen useless mission statements posted inside lobbies, or laminated and decaying inside desks, never to be heard from again by anyone, especially top leaders who forced that type of drivel on the organization to begin with. That is not what we are aiming for here.

As with much of what you will learn in this book, demand creation is an intentional *design* initiative. With this in mind, relative to designing unprecedented value, determining "what to do" hinges on eight critical elements:

1. Leadership's conviction to live the purpose and core behaviors (foundation)

2. Rally the organization around the higher calling (communication of "Why")
3. See what others miss by discovering "unspoken" customer needs (ethnography)
4. Find the common threads from #3, detecting insights (beyond observations)
5. Identify the MVA (minimal viable audience)
6. Determine what offerings can and should be developed (consider co-creation)
7. Build emotionally exciting experiences into offerings (merge with functionality)
8. Execute! (who does what by when?)

Please note that #6, if not the entire list, will be given greater focus in Chapter 14, *Component Four: Designing "Priceless."*

#8 above, Execution, is often the bane of well-intending companies, especially those of an entrepreneurial nature. They are great at ideation and "starting things," but lack the grit and process mindset – not to mention the experience – to execute effectively. Said another way, the vast majority of entrepreneurs not only suck at management – the execution of the necessary daily operational activities –

they steer as far away from it as possible. "Management" is not exciting enough, it cannot hold their interest, even though that is what separates the successful enterprise from the trash heap. Creativity and innovation are critically important, but without rock solid management the company will fail fast.

Therefore, since the topic of execution has been captured so wonderfully in other books and places, please refer to the following list for assistance:

- **W. Edwards Deming.** Plan – Do – Check (Study) – Act. Also, Deming's famed *14 Points For Management* stands the test of time, and is still applicable today. (see Appendix A at the end of this book).
- **S.M.A.R.T. Objectives.** Specific; Measurable; Attainable; Relevant; Time-bound
- *Execution: The Discipline of Getting Things Done.* A staple of execution, Larry Bossidy and Ram Charan hit a home run.
- *The Seven Habits of Highly Effective People.* Stephen Covey. Iconic.
- *The Four Disciplines of Execution: Achieving Your Wildly Important Goals.* Sean Covey and Chris McChesney may have provided the best guide to date.

- ***Getting Things Done.*** No list on the topic of execution is complete without David Allen, a leading expert on personal and organizational productivity.

Additionally, regarding the design of effective game plans, please be aware that there are two saboteurs lurking within organizations, constantly plotting to destroy any chance of success: permissiveness and irresponsibility. To overcome these villains, a regimen of *discipline* and *accountability* must become institutionalized. Without this regimen, sustaining a thriving demand creation culture is near impossible.

Keep project teams small and autonomous

Nothing stalls progress faster than bureaucracy. Whatever the reason a group is formed – to tackle short or long term problems, or investigate something new – try to cap the participants at five. At that number, any potential politicking is kept at bay, and speed and agility become the norm. Also, there can never be a deadlocked vote.

If an organization is one that is crafted with professionalism, trust and "fit," then ad hoc teams should be encouraged to tackle anything and everything – permission not needed. As long as leadership has clearly communicated the purpose (reason why the company exists and the difference it's trying to make in people's lives) and mission (core strategy that fulfills the purpose), then people should be free to mobilize at a moment's notice, able to cross departmental lines without interference, and *get things done*. These "skunk works" should be celebrated, praise given liberally to foster the spirit of innovation.

The more teams that exist, the greater degree of execution and results are achieved. Which leads us into to our next chapter.

NOTE: If leadership fears this type of self-governing, nimble structure, then either insecure or dictatorial leadership is present, or the organization hired its charges poorly. Whichever the case, replacement is warranted, and should occur quickly. It will take far too long and too much money to try and implement "change management."

Chapter 10

Culpable:

Accountable Execution

"It is wrong and immoral to seek to escape the consequences of one's acts"

~ Mahatma Gandhi

"Accountability is the measure of a leader's height"

~ Jeffrey Benjamin

"99% of all failures come from people who have a habit of making excuses"

~ George Washington Carver

"Um, yeah. What they said."

~ Sean Stormes

Who will do what by when?

Seems fair and easy, right? Well, not exactly. Here is the truth that some leaders are uncomfortable with: What are the consequences for non-performance? What *is* non-performance? Has it been clearly defined, measured and shared? The organization is only as strong as what leadership will and will not tolerate. The moment people, particularly senior leaders, fail to execute as outlined in Chapter 9, *Wisdom: Choosing the Most Effective Game Plan*, a precedent is set – and that is a dangerous, slippery slope that is difficult to recover from.

Every problem I have seen or experienced in business can be attributed directly to leadership – NOT the people doing the work. In other words, the "heavy lifting" of accountability should be owned by top executives – to be clear, the CEO or business owner – not the rank and file. Why? Because employees do not create the rules, processes or environment – the entire system and design of how "work" occurs. Rather, it is *leadership* that creates the system, and then asks others to succeed within that system. As you have heard many times, if you place good people into a bad system, the system wins every time.

Therefore, it is leadership's responsibility to design systems that allow people to win.

Why, then, do senior leaders shirk this responsibility? It is because many have misguided belief systems, thinking that most problems, errors and mistakes are due to people, which is 100% false as Dr. Deming and others have proven. Problems are caused by the system, which leadership and management designed, develop and own. Another reason why some top dogs will not accept responsibility is because they enjoy playing the blame game. It is easier on them that way, and aligns with their monomaniacal ego. Accepting responsibility for the system takes a lot of work, and many at the top are work-averse. Many designed their companies as a "lifestyle business," one that allows them ample free time while others toil away in bad systems. Fair? I think not. Reprehensible? Offensive? You betcha.

Accountable Execution means that senior leadership should be liable for the company's performance. How can an organization be truly "fit" if top management is not leading each day's principled and guiding "calisthenics?" The last thing leadership wants is a flabby, out of shape and underperforming enterprise, yet all too often they are truant, especially in the small and mid-market arenas. Conversely, at high performing companies, one will almost always find a senior leadership team – led by an obsessed, 100% committed and present CEO – that is ultra-engaged in constantly improving the business ecosystem so the company and its people can flourish. They see their role as one of being an exemplary steward of purpose, responsible for both profitability and purpose fulfillment.

While these Level 5 leaders are expert at getting things done through others, they are omnipresent, keeping a persistent, watchful eye over the organization. They know that the buck stops with them, and welcome, embrace and protect that accountability more than anyone else. The result is that employees recognize that behavior, and being acting like owners themselves.

Accountable Execution is a primary key to achieving elite, system-wide organizational performance, particularly in the most important areas of demand creation and PRG.

Section III

The Seven Components of Demand Creation

Chapter 11

Component One:

Got Purpose? (Part II)

"Efforts and courage are not enough without purpose and direction"

~ John F. Kennedy, 35th U.S. President

"Purpose is not separate from the operating business plan. Rather, it is the hub of the operating business plan."

~ Sean Stormes

Picking up where we left off in Chapter 7, *Linchpin: Got Purpose (Part I)*, I believe the reason why purpose has not become the norm in business – the fact that most senior leadership teams do not see or believe the powerful demand creation nature of the beast – is because the term has become misconstrued, and synonymous with, "social responsibility."

While social responsibility is both admirable and much needed (see TOMS shoes, for example), purpose can and should possess more "institutional horsepower" to the business's day-to-day decision-making. In the Revenution, purpose becomes the *operating theme* – the business plan's core and common thread outlining how the organization wins, particularly with PRG.

Similarly, great stewards of purpose tend to be charismatic and resolute in their beliefs, injecting the organization with an infectious and exciting passion around the higher calling. And, these stewards know that breathing purpose "life" into the company must occur before setting expectations of external impact. Since there are no companies – only people – it is employees who are ultimately accountable to fulfilling the purpose. But if they do not know why purpose is the linchpin, or develop a strong belief system around purpose, then it begins to feel like an imposition. And once people feeling like they're being told to do something "Because I said so," passive aggressive behavior develops at best, sabotage occurs at worst.

NOTE: Purpose should be focused *externally* (impacting people), though its primary utility is *internal* – serving as organizational True North.

Clean Slate Wisdom: There is a dangerous land mine to avoid when forging purpose. Above all else, purpose cannot be 100% aspirational. Rather, this is an endeavor of excavation, drilling and tunneling into the organization's past to identify the secret sauce that allows it to succeed. If "proof of sauce" is not evident, then it is merely aspirational – a death sentence when shaping True North. Without *purpose authenticity*, the business plan is negatively impacted right from the start.

Six Steps to Forging Purpose, the "Higher Institutional Calling"

Please keep in mind what needs to be accomplished: Break from the competitive herd of sameness. *Create insane demand.* It's time to get granular on this most important topic.

- **Authenticity.** What is rooted in the organization's DNA? Look to the past. Why was the company founded? What problem(s) would it solve, and how?

- **Big Idea.** Must get larger than mission and deeper than vision, though each has its place. What is the central idea that people will rally around? What's the cause? Some refer to it as a "brand ideal." People want to know what you stand for. Take your customer to an *impossible* place. It is a compliment if people say, "That doesn't make any sense."

- **Challenge.** Does it confront and denounce conventional wisdom, blowing up anything related to the status quo? Mission and vision often lack the stuff of revolution, so be bold! Pick a fight and force people to choose sides.

- **Clarity.** Higher causes cannot be vague or bland. To matter – to have a substantial and measurable impact on all stakeholders – higher causes must be crisp, succinct and sharply defined. *Concise.* To solve an organizational identity crisis, purpose must inform people of who and what the organization is, and what it is not.

- **Coherent.** How does purpose become *pervasive*? Institutionalized? That is the only way to have substantive impact.

- **Inspirational.** Forget motivation. That is for six year-olds. Does it "grab the soul," inspire the desired behavior, and define how all decisions will be made?

Examples of Elite and Effective Purpose Statements

Here are 13 outstanding purpose statements that serve as the operating guide to some very successful organizations, each an elite demand creator. Notice that each statement has a dominant, strong verb that elicits high emotion, and makes it clear as to the "Who." Each also knows exactly what daunting problem is trying to solve.

- **Whole Foods Market:** "Changing how America eats."

- **ArrivedOutdoors:** "To help transitioning business owners find their 'next'"

- **Johnson and Johnson:** "To alleviate pain and suffering"

- **Dimensional Innovations:** "Liberating people from mediocre experiences"

- **Disney:** "Using our imaginations to bring happiness to millions"

- **Redemption Plus:** "Enriching lives through insights that empower"

- **Southwest Airlines:** "To give people the freedom to fly"

- **CrossFirst Bank:** "Serving people in extraordinary ways"

- **Charles Schwab:** "A relentless ally for the individual investor"

- ✓ **BUCS Analytics:** "In dogged pursuit of eradicating bad business decisions"

- ✓ **BMW:** "To enable people to experience the joy of driving"

- ✓ **American Red Cross:** "Enabling Americans to perform extraordinary acts in the face of emergencies"

- ✓ **Tobii Dynavox:** "100,000 voices"

Every single decision, large and small, should sufficiently answer *just one question*, simultaneously reducing massive amounts of waste, rework, time and effort, making life much more simple:

> *"Does it help fulfill the purpose?"*

Take an Important Cue From TV's *Homeland*

In this Emmy and Golden Globe-award winning series, starring Claire Danes and Mandy Patinkin as key players in the often dark and mysterious world of the CIA, the agency is constantly and forever *recruiting assets* to further their cause and ensure victory.

To protect against potential negativity or apathy, and secure necessary deep-seated belief, recruiting assets on the purpose front is no different. Therefore, how is senior leadership identifying its advocates and promoters, and enlisting them in the cause? Peers often find more credibility in other peers vs. bosses, and besides, it is the employees who are the foundation of organizational fitness and demand creation.

In fact, when undertaking any major initiative, always recruit assets first.

Chapter 12

Component Two:

The Village People

"We see our customers as invited guests to a party, and we are the hosts"

~ Jeff Bezos, founder and CEO of Amazon

"Who are you worthy of leading, and why should you matter to them?"

~ Sean Stormes

You can read in many other places about the importance of identifying the "ideal client," so in addition to all of that content, I ask that you trust me when I share the most important component the usual-suspect-gurus *miss*:

> **Having real purpose dramatically changes the ideal customer profile**

In fact, not only will the profile change, but the actual people will begin looking more like "dream customers." Therefore, let's start referring to your village as exactly that: *Dream Customers*. After all, the higher the bar, the greater chance you have of defeating sameness and achieving attraction. Additionally, try not to confuse a village of dream customers with a traditional "target market." The type of village we desire seeks a strong emotional connection with a movement or cause, not rote products or services.

How Well Do You Really Know Your Dream Customer?

Every business or organization should discover its unique *Dream Customer formula*, because without it, PRG can never be maximized, meaning demand creation becomes nothing more than a pipe dream.

Therefore, how much ethnography has been performed with customers and prospects, as in "live and in person?" What are the no trade-off key qualifiers, attributes and traits that forge discipline when choosing business partners? How will these qualifiers be used for the greatest impact? What happens to existing customers who don't measure up? What does it all *mean*?

Companies that ignore this important business tenet often wallow in the poor marketplace position of being all things to all people – intentionally or not – ultimately standing for nothing, placing them at a substantial competitive disadvantage (unless the entire industry is living in a world of sameness). To be blunt, just because someone can write a check does not mean they are good for business. Often, when doing business with misaligned partners, that check results in a "minus profitability" scenario, costing the enterprise more than what was paid for the product or service.

To achieve clarity on this issue, do any of the following examples resonate with you?

Customers who ...

- Never seem to be satisfied – always complaining – no matter what is done to try and please them, consistently devouring valuable and costly resources (people; time; money).

- Habitually pay late, negatively impacting cash flow, causing (bank) lines of credit to be accessed, therefore incurring costly interest and the inability to use funds elsewhere (and faster) for the greater good of the organization.

- Do not give a rip about quality, excellent guest experience or other value drivers that can positively impact the customer's organization, instead choosing to beat suppliers down on price at every turn, which only serves to make their providers weaker in every aspect.

- Either don't understand or care about win-win business partnership scenarios to ensure that their providers are profitable, sustainable and continuously improving, ultimately helping customers fortify *their* purpose and *their* profitability.

Whether the enterprise is a non-profit, small or midmarket business, or division of the Fortune 500, chances are high that the "hidden costs" within the firm are eroding hard-earned profits by the minute. These expenses don't show up on any specific line item within the Balance Sheet, Income Statement or P&L. They may wear deceiving clothing like "Direct Labor Cost," or "Expedited Shipping," or simply additional head count necessary to handle the residue from the four bullet points above. Waste and rework is a primary killer of companies, and its "invisibility suit" can not only be maddening for leadership – *often wondering why gross profit isn't higher* – but because its hidden identity causes leadership to squeeze profits from otherwise innocent areas that can severely damage the organization's value proposition.

Clean Slate Wisdom: When choosing Dream Customers, the most important qualifier is, "Do they believe what YOU believe?" If they do not, variation is exponentially increased, causing expensive waste and rework, eroding profits. This proves, once again, that organizational fitness is directly correlated to P&L performance. As important, there are scores of people – and probably entire villages – who are at this very moment scanning the horizon to locate the type of purpose you have discovered (or will discover, right?), and wish to align. Said another way, one of the best ways to increase PRG in the next 12 months is to *let people know what you stand for*. (For assistance, please refer to Chapter 16: *Captivation*)

Chick-fil-A: PRG Stake Firmly Planted In Ground

How important is it to your PRG efforts to let people know what you stand for – to firmly plant your "Conviction Stake" in the ground? Case in point: *Chick-fil-A*.

In 2012, when then-President and now CEO Dan Cathy said on a radio show – then shortly thereafter reaffirmed in an article by the *Baptist Press* – that he and his organization believed in the biblical definition of marriage, that between a man and a woman, the national backlash from the LGBT community (and other special interest groups) was enormous. Boycotts were called for, and an overwhelming amount of negative press ensued. One might think that this dilemma spelled doom for the high-flying restaurant chain.

Guess again.

Regardless of your personal beliefs on the topic, please notice what happens when villages are evident, rallied behind an organization's higher calling. While those who opposed Chick-fil-A protested and voted with their wallets accordingly, the company's raving fans showed up in droves to support the beleaguered CEO and restaurant chain. You would have probably guessed those two outcomes. What's important to recognize, though, is that the rest of the population *that didn't know what the company stood for* – and agreed with the stance – came out of the woodwork to show support. Take a look at the company's performance directly after the PR flap:

Chick-fil-A™ PR Results: Q3 2012 vs. Q3 2011

Consumer use .... +2.2%

Ad awareness .... +6.5%

Market share .... +0.6%

Regular customer base broadened ...... + 28 out of 35 states

Source: *USA Today, Bruce Horowitz, October 24, 2012*

Apparently, achieving polarization due to the design, development and delivery of real purpose can be *good* for business, contrary to popular belief. My advice: *Stop playing it safe.*

Discovering Your Dream Customer

The following five steps can put you on the path to discovering your Dream Customer. Please use this list to build a viable Dream Customer profile, and apply it diligently and with conviction when qualifying business partners, allowing no exceptions.

1. **Do they believe what YOU believe?** I am repeating this, and for good reason. Natural groupings occur when similar beliefs are evident. Like a moth to a flame, people are drawn to ideologies they believe in and possess strong conviction for, therefore your Big Idea (Chapter 13: *Monopoly, Anyone?*) must be just that: a real game-changer. This is where ethnography becomes invaluable. The most successful organizations understand and know, on a deep level, their dream customers *99% better than the competition.*

2. **Start with the MVA.** If you try to attack a village that is too large from the outset, chances of success are greatly diminished. Better to start with an MVA, or minimal viable audience. This may feel counterintuitive, but the

trick is to find a group of people who believe that your offering is special, as in *unprecedented value* special. Remember, we are not after sameness or incremental growth here. The objective is to create insane demand – to "attract," transforming into the most powerful of magnets. Thus, when getting started, you may have little to offer and few resources available to make sufficient noise. The solution is to identify a narrow group – just a sliver of the entire pie – with specific demographics, psychographics and a specific problem. Only then can raving fans be cultivated and consistently harvested. Reach can always be expanded after gaining traction.

3. **Identify what prospects hold providers accountable to.** Many prospects will answer with a shrug or trite commentary, and that will tip you off quickly: "This is not my Dream Customer." Conversely, when answers are more elegant, aligned and thought provoking, then everything possible should be done to form an alliance. When Dream Customer prospects value these types of questions and general interest, they will often try hard to find a way to say 'yes.'

4. **Mention "co-creation" and "co-destiny," and pay close attention to how they react.** Those who value true business partnerships make it clear that success strategies are a two-way street, often seeking opportunities to work together with disparate resources.

What happens once my village is clearly defined and identified?

- **Incite a movement and fan the flames.** When I escaped the corporate world in late 2008, I had nothing but knowledge, a firm belief in my proprietary PRG architecture, and a wealth of faith that I could succeed (there was also decades of experience and proven results – I was not a novice). Quickly, I drew a loud and provocative line in the sand, making it very clear what I believed in, and what I railed (hard) against. This seemed refreshing to CEOs and business owners who thought their only hope for significant PRG hinged on salespeople, sales training firms and marketing agencies. They had never met a *Master Demand Creator*.

- **The Bullhorn Effect.** I drew that line in the sand with the most effective and disruptive bullhorn I could find, and it went way beyond social media, which I also took advantage of (as you are aware, technology has allowed everyone the opportunity to be discovered, to let their village know that they exist and why they matter). I approached my local Business Journal newspaper, shared my unprecedented value, and for the next seven years helped senior leadership create demand in a highly viewed, bi-monthly *Growth Strategies* column. In fact, the column eventually went national into 40+ markets. Think "earned media," because nobody is going to hand you a damn thing. NOTE: It is important to realize that every village is also a potential bullhorn, sharing with others the experience, benefits and sheer pleasure of your valuable offering.

- **Mobilize the troops.** The next objective is to mobilize the Dream Customer village, bringing them together to *forge community*. Public speaking, workshops and meet ups are great ways to rally, excite and inspire the gang. And, as I am sure you've guessed, you can mobilize the village online too by assembling via blogs and podcasts, soliciting participation and feedback. This component is critical because, as we know, there is power and strength in numbers. It probably comes as no surprise, then, that I began speaking all over the country to develop the aforementioned community. After all, you're reading this book, aren't you?

- **Admit who's really in charge and care for them.** Recognize that you do not own the village. Rather, they own you. They cannot be told what to do, a type of check and balance to those whom the village follows. Screw up, and the village jettisons the leader, often silently. Nurture your village and the "family" will reward you ten-fold.

The Never-Ending Story

I can tell you from experience that this exercise is never complete. As an organization evolves, this model will evolve as well, but perhaps the continual process of discovery is just as important as what is discovered.

Chapter 13

Component Three:

Monopoly, Anyone?

"The critical thing about these monopolies is, it's not enough to have a monopoly for just a moment"

~ Peter Thiel, PayPal co-founder and author of *Zero to One*

"Be the only ones who do what you do"

~ Sean Stormes

Referring to Chapter 1, *Anemia: 11 Causes of Poor PRG*, the emperor often has no clothes, meaning the value proposition is shoddy at best, entirely void of value at worst. Exacerbating the problem is *fear*, which just happens to be Point 8 in *Deming's 14 Points For Management*. No one will tell the CEO the bad though truthful news about the naked value proposition, and if they do, they are often rebuffed, or worse, labeled forever more as a malcontent, their career poisoned beyond repair. The perceived risk far outweighs the reward, so silence envelops the kingdom.

If you do not believe you or your organization can become the only ones who do what you do, then you are already doomed to an existence of sameness, with all of the warts and ugly P&Ls that come with that dark territory.

The Genesis of Game Changing Big Ideas

Zipcar. AirBnB. PayPal. Cirque de Soleil. Atlassian. Wegman's. Netflix. Quick Trip. The list of Big Idea companies and organizations grows by the day, limited only by imagination, critical thinking and boldness. But what are the building blocks of elite Big Idea design? Before answering that question, we need context.

In a December 2016 Wall Street Journal article by Greg Ip entitled, *The Economy's Hidden Problem: We're Out of Big Ideas,* Ip poses this provocative question:

Dwindling gains in science, medicine and technology hold back growth; is America too risk-averse?

The implication of this notion is also captured in Ip's writing: *"By all appearances, we're in a golden age of innovation. Every month sees new advances in artificial intelligence, gene therapy, robotics and software apps. Research and development as a share of gross domestic product is near an all-time high. There are more scientists and engineers in the U.S. than ever before. Yet none of this has translated into meaningful advances in Americans' standard of living."*

"Meaningful advances in American's standard of living." Could it be possible that Ip's "golden age of innovation" statement points to lack of purpose within most organizations, causing the dearth of Big Ideas? The converse suggests that innovation becomes merely incremental – therefore not improving people's lives – when bold purpose is absent. And when bold purpose is absent, *Small Ideas* become the norm.

Not only does the economy struggle when this occurs, but obviously America's companies do, too. As always, look no further than leadership as the culprit.

Five Signs That You Are Ready to Forge a Big Idea

1. **The status quo pisses you off.** Conventionalism nags at you, eating away at your common sense all hours of the day and night. The screaming inside your head says, "There has to be a better way!" And when you hear accepted, usual-suspect-gurus spew their supposed "wisdom," you react with, "That is such bullshit. Been there, done that, and nothing changed."

2. **You have (finally) rejected the belief that the sales organization, including selling skills, is a panacea for PRG.** *Please.* You have read the first 12 chapters, right? Incremental growth is the enemy of demand creation. When was the last time your sales team single handedly un-evened the competitive playing field? Or were they just trying to grow sales incrementally (at best) – "hit their number" – with a naked emperor? If you keep wondering why improving revenue is a maddening, daily exercise, then you're ready for a Big Idea.

3. **You have (finally) rejected the belief that hipster branding is the answer.** *Please* ... times TWO. The old adage that marketers don't like to share is, "Marketing works 50% of the time. We just don't know which 50%." And in the world of branding, that adage becomes even more convoluted. Purpose *is* the brand, and it is revealed in how the company operates, eventually shining through in its products, services and experiences.

4. **Ethnography efforts reveal the same recurring "unspoken" problem.** Your "scouts," whom we'll discuss in greater detail in Chapters 14 and 18, fill their advance reporting with a persistent and lingering theme: Customers and prospects are experiencing an annoyance that seems ripe for solving, yet no one is addressing it.

5. **There is strong evidence that the organization has become purpose-driven.** Once the movement becomes palpable, and there is a discernable, innate desire to improve people's lives, then the troops are ready to tackle the world. If the movement is not palpable, leadership has much work to do to realize the desired state; a higher calling.

Peter Thiel and the Topic of Monopolies

There may be no better book on the topic of devising monopolies than Peter Thiel's (and Blake Masters) *Zero To One: Notes to Startups, or How to Build the Future*. Please review the following excerpts:

- "If you're the founder/entrepreneur starting a company, you always want to aim for monopoly and avoid competition. There are exactly two kinds of businesses in this world: Businesses that are perfectly competitive and businesses that are monopolies."
- "If you get a creative monopoly for inventing something new, I think it's symptomatic of having created something really valuable."
- "Anyone that has a monopoly will pretend that they're in incredible competition." (this keeps the fire burning, and keeps them honest and humble)
- "The founder must always be super-mindful that there are very powerful incentives to distort the nature of these markets."
- "Almost all successful companies in Silicon Valley had some model of starting with small markets and expanding. If the initial market at Facebook was 10,000 people at

Harvard, it then went from 0 to 60% market share in 10 days. That was a very auspicious start."
- "I think all happy companies are different, because they are doing something very unique. All unhappy companies are alike, because they fail to escape the essential sameness which is competition."
- "My somewhat arbitrary rule of thumb is you want to have a technology that's an order of magnitude better than the next best thing, as in 10X better."
- "The thing about network effects is that they are often very hard to get started."
- "I always think in some ways, the better framing is … you want to be the last mover. You want to be the last company in a category."
- "One of the things we overvalue in Silicon Valley is growth rates and we undervalue durability."
- "Scientists never make any money. They're always diluted into thinking that they live in a just universe that'll reward them for their work."
- "Vertical integration is sort of a very under explored modality of technological progress that people would do well to look at more."
- "There is something about the world of bits, as opposed to the world of atoms, where you can often get very fast adoption."

- "It's not that when lots of people are trying to do something, that that's proof of it being valuable. I think that when lots of people are trying to do something, that is often proof of insanity."
- "Don't always go through the tiny little door that everyone is trying to rush through. Maybe go around the corner and go through the vast gate that no one's taking."

And … My Top Six Quotes From *Zero to One*

- "Today's 'best practices' lead to dead ends; the best paths are new and untried"
- "Brilliant thinking is rare, but *courage* is in even shorter supply than genius"
- "Question ideas and rethink business from scratch"
- "It is better to risk boldness than triviality"
- "If your product requires advertising or salespeople, to sell it, it's not good enough"
- "The best entrepreneur knows this: Every great business is built on a secret that's hidden from the outside world," he says.

Increasing the Chances of Realizing a Monopoly: Seek Small Villages

It bears repeating that focusing on an MVA (or "MVV" in this case, a minimal viable village) greatly increases the odds of forging a sustainable monopoly. Conversely, to exist as a mere kernel in a vast cornfield, where there is a massive audience craving corn, is not advisable.

Inventing an attractive category seizes the undivided attention of an otherwise ignored small village. Captivating the neglected eyeballs, ears and hearts of prospective devotees is an honor and comes with great responsibility. These are people who pine to believe in "something more," and are vulnerable as a result. Be empathetic toward their circumstance, behave responsibly, and PRG is yours for the taking.

Additionally, a monopoly can cruise beneath the radar of potential raiders, those who may eventually realize, and take offense to, their status quo apple (cash) cart being upset. For a while, at least, the monopolistic organization can work unnoticed and uninterrupted, continuously improving and honing its unprecedented value.

Beware, though. If the leader betrays the village, then members' attention will be diverted elsewhere, most likely never to return. That betrayal can take the form of violating the purpose and core behaviors – the "promise" – often chasing the almighty dollar, becoming vanilla in the process. The kiss of death is to forget that in the Revenution, a demand creator is one who stands for something bold and meaningful. Promises of this magnitude should be kept, not broken. Behave accordingly.

Chapter 14

Component Four:

Designing "Priceless"

"To harvest the power of design thinking, individuals, teams, and whole organizations have to cultivate optimism."

~ Tim Brown, CEO, IDEO; author of *Change by Design: How Design Thinking Transforms Organizations and Inspires Innovation*

"Linear thinking is about sequences; mind maps are about connections."

~ Tim Brown

"There is nothing more frustrating than coming up with the right answer to the wrong question."

~ Tim Brown

"Unprecedented value is derived from seeing what other miss – the 'unspoken' need'"

~ Sean Stormes

Do you and your organization desire a market position where premium pricing, exceptional customer loyalty, robust job creation and remarkable PRG are the norm? If this is your quest, then demand creation and the resulting Attraction Model is your salvation, and may best be explained by a story from the insipid world of automobile manufacturing.

In the late spring of 2016, a car company began receiving $1,000 deposits for the firm's new, mid-market sedan. People waited in long lines for hours to happily hand over their money for the $38,000 vehicle. To provide context, there were no:

- Big PR splashes
- Traditional marketing gimmicks
- Dealerships (to speak of)
- Pricing games
- SALESPEOPLE (!)

And best of all ... wait for it ... *there was no car*. That's right – no physical, actual product to sell. The sedan was not due for two more years. *What the hell?* conventional automakers thought. How did this happen? Who does that? Who *buys* like that?

To help answer those questions, here is one of the most important, provocative and beneficial questions you can ask of your senior leadership:

> **What high value does the organization provide *independent* of the core product or service?**

"Independent" infers attraction beyond functional benefits. The idea is to initially design with human emotion first – to determine how your stuff will matter to people on a deep level. How is "uncommon care" baked into the offering? Most often, people buy emotionally and rationalize the purchase decision later. One of the many reasons Tesla has been successful is because the company has 'secret' insights such as fashion awareness of its customers (e.g. Leonardo diCaprio). This is a great example of seeing what others miss.

Additionally, stop doing what the sales training industry prescribes, which is to "identify pain," i.e. the spoken need, by asking customers archaic questions like, "What keeps you up at night?" or "How can I save you time and money?" The customer can only tell you what they know – the surface answer that routinely bubbles up because they have been asked about their pain a million times by the same schlep salespeople. They struggle to clearly and succinctly articulate their daily hassles that, cumulatively, make their lives complex and rife with hassle. This exasperated state makes it hard to explain what the root causes of the hassle map are. It takes a master ethnographer to "see what others miss" and uncover the holy grail of monopoly creation: The primary *unspoken* need.

History is littered with wildly successful ideas and inventions that no one clamored for; there was no palpable want or need, merely a silent yet mammoth void that few were able to see.

Clean Slate Wisdom: No one asked for the automobile, airplane, radio, television or Internet, to name just five. There was no massive demand, no whining or pining for any of these things. Rather, someone saw what others missed, considered the unspoken needs of an oft-ignored customer, then designed, developed and delivered unprecedented value. Do not ignore that which you see out of the corner of your eye. Developing this type of X-ray vision should be a key objective for anyone tasked with demand creation.

Creating Institutional Obsession

I have spent months, sometimes years working with organizations that claim their cultures are "this" or "that," and I've struggled to see, or more importantly *feel* it. Aspirational or anointed claims of culture identity can do extreme damage to demand creation efforts. What often happens is the CEO falls in love with the ideology of a particular attribute or movement – think "Innovation" or "Conscious Capitalism" or "Happiness" – and actually believes their culture reflects the chosen dogma. Of course, nothing is further from the truth, and because employees do not feel it either, nothing changes. And if nothing changes, sameness rules and any hope of demand creation is lost.

This is simply another rendition of The Emperor (culture, in this case) Has No Clothes.

Rather, demand creation requires *Proof of Obsession* from the top dog. Actions speak louder than words. Is the CEO's obsession 100% aligned with the purpose and core behaviors, and does the operational business plan flow directly from it? Is the top dog truant or present? Since we are dealing with such a high bar, is the top dog omnipresent? If not, how else can a Big Idea take root, be cultivated and eventually harvested? How else can a monopoly be forged? Industries are disrupted and new, lucrative categories are created by virtue of obsessed senior leadership – not those who have designed a "lifestyle business." Obsession cannot be delegated. It must be modeled from the top and baked into the both the operating plan and associated behaviors, with a heavy emphasis on traditional HR model redesign (see Chapter 21, *Full Integration: Baking the New Model Into The Company's Bones*).

Does the obsession resonate internally to the degree that it is significantly "revealed" externally with all whom the organization touches? If not, how can a business owner truly say that they care deeply about customers – more so than anyone on the planet – to the point of creating insane demand?

Ethnography: The Most Sought After Skill

It is all starts with a person, an unaddressed problem, an associated unspoken need to solve, and a Big Idea. How do these factors interact in complex, unpredictable and counterintuitive ways? The objective is not to try to convince, persuade or cajole people into buying something (selling!). Rather, how can you appeal to the "human condition" that compels The Village People to "want" or "desire?"

Consider Dan Brown's 2003 runaway bestseller, *The Da Vinci Code*, where the cryptex was first introduced. The portable vault was used to hide secret messages, protecting valuable information written on the contained scroll – the codex. Once unlocked, after all of the necessary parts click perfectly into place, the secret messages were revealed. In our case, that would be the unspoken needs that allow for the design of unprecedented value.

Ethnography is understanding, on a deep level, the *mechanics* of an organization's ecosystem – "how the work gets done" – and the associated headaches, annoyances and inconveniences. Watch closely how people behave in their natural element. Ask challenging, insightful questions, behaving like a curious child. Soak up every nuance that is uttered, being in the moment, mindful of seeing and feeling, employing critical thinking to arrive at theories and potential insights – the gas that makes the demand creation engine purr.

Clean Slate Wisdom: To become a top Demand Creator, leadership and its charges must learn to become highly *sentient*, transforming into scouts and hunters, finding what others have missed. Soon, others will see this behavior from the top – along with clear expectations to do the same – and will begin acting in kind. Forging a culture of curiosity correlates directly to healthy P&Ls.

The Value Design Flow Map: Uncovering Valuable Insights That Lead to Unprecedented Value

1. Questions
→ 2. Observations
→ 3. Identify Common Themes (analysis/connect dots)
→ 4. Develop Insights/New Truths
→ 5. Design Unprecedented Value
→ 6 Test
→ 7. Customer Confirm/Validate
→ 8. Benchmark KPIs
→ 9. Launch New Offerings
→ 10. Assess Results
→ 11. Find the Trigger
→ 12. PRG!

1. Design **questions** that will allow you to "see/understand what others don't (or can't or won't)."

2. Mindfulness. Ethnography. *LEARN*. Collect **observations** and submit to a central holding tank.

3. **Analysis.** Connect the dots. Identify common themes. *What does it all mean?*

4. Determine new truths ... **insights**! What prevailing industry assumptions and conventional wisdom are being challenged?

5. Design **unprecedented value**. What new contributions will you make? How will the new, subsequent offerings **empower** the customer?

6. Perform **testing**. "Plan - Do - Study - Act" (Rinse and Repeat; it's a never-ending cycle of improvement)

7. Customer **confirm** and **validate**. Also consider co-creation / co-destiny. In other words, be sure any new offerings are **"customer certified"** before launching on a grand scale.

8. Determine and **benchmark** key performance indicators (KPIs) before launch, including <u>metrics and measurements</u>. What should improve, and why? What are the desired results?

9. **Introduce** new offerings to the marketplace. Ensure that awesome **marketing** is employed to generate necessary buzz and attraction.

10. **Assess** effectiveness. What's the report card (<u>results</u>) based on the <u>data</u>?

11. Find the **triggers.** Once the offering is launched, the team must continuously determine how fast they can improve. There is a considerable distance between what customers purchase and what they really desire. This is how to keep the imitators at arm's length.

Why Understanding Societal and Cultural Shifts Are Necessary For Designing "Priceless"

While ethnography is integral to identifying insights that can drive innovative, unprecedented value, understanding why *marketplace shifts* occur is equally important. Paying close attention to human environs – keeping tabs on subtle trends – can make or break demand creation strategies. Appreciating, recognizing and interpreting nascent movements are indispensable.

Who is tasked with trend watching in your organization? How is it performed? Is it part of the operating plan, complete with allocated resources (as part of the "growth budget"), or is it on the periphery of core strategy, destined to become an afterthought?

Here is a partial list of what trend spotters should be on the lookout for – the categories that often experience subtle shifts. Those who capitalize on the MVV within these shifting categories win big.

- Financial
- Emotional

- Communication styles and methods
- Fashion
- Social norms
- Product, service and experience design

Big Idea Architecture

Design and engineer your unprecedented value offering to ensure that it is …

1. **Provocative.** Can your Big Idea challenge and inspire, to the point of *offending* some people – because if no one hates it, no one will love it? How much dialogue will it cause within your MVV, then outward to the fringe – and possibly beyond? HINT: If people in the industry remark, "That just doesn't make any sense," you are on the right track.

2. **Seductive.** Does it produce an enchanting connection that forges human attachment, to the point of devotion? There is a plethora of emotional real estate to capture within your MVV, and the first to secure it, wins.

3. **Exciting.** What makes the pulse quicken? What captures the imagination? Why do people stand in line for the newest Apple or Tesla product, or the opening of the latest Chick-fil-A?

4. **Efficient.** Wasting time and money is at the top of most people's frustrations, as is accepting more risk than they can tolerate.

5. **Empowering.** People don't want to be told what to do – they want choices; the ability to customize – *personalize* – their own experience.

6. **Ridiculously Simple.** Is automation part of the offering, or clarity where complexity current resides (consider complex or poorly written instructions)?

7. **Agile.** Is it easy? Convenient? Fast? Nimble? *Athletic*? The opposite of agile is cable companies and airlines – take your pick.

> **Clean Slate Wisdom:** Exceptional demand creators infuse first-class functionality with emotional excitement. This is a "quantum improvement." Think of any category-killing, game-changing product or service, and this has been the case – without exception. As Peter Thiel has said, "I am personally skeptical of all the Lean Startup methodology. I think the really great companies did something that was sort of a quantum improvement that really differentiated them."

If Technology Is At The Core, Then Be Sure It Is Proprietary and Valuable to the MVV

Technology must be significantly better – Thiel says "at least 10 times better" – than its closest substitute in some key aspect to lead to a real monopolistic advantage. If that does not happen, it may provide only short-term, incremental advantage. Compare this requirement to the companies you know well, and that have dominated their respective industries:

- Google's search
- Betterment, Wealthfront and Blooom's financial planning algorithms
- Paypal's online payment
- Netflix' recommendation engine ("Since you liked that, you might like this")
- Amazon's inventory behemoth
- Apple's user experience and design

Case Study: Atlassian

If you have never heard of growth hacking – a valuable tool in the demand creator's toolbox – then you don't know what you're messing. Growth hacking means designing attraction into your product or service so that you don't have to waste time, effort and dollars selling or advertising it. Need proof?

Atlassian, a $5 billion project management and chat apps B2B software company, had $320 million in sales in 2015, and pushed $450 million in 2016. More than 80 Fortune 100 companies use Atlassian's software. Oh, and did I mention they don't have any salespeople? They've *never* had any salespeople. And their competitors are experiencing high anxiety over it.

From a May 18, 2016 Bloomberg Business article (Dina Bass, reporting; https://bloom.bg/2j4FVrB):

"Brandon Cipes, vice president for information systems at OceanX, has spent enough time in senior IT positions to hate sales calls. 'It's like buying a car—a process that seemingly should be so simple, but every time I have to, it's like a five- to six-hour ordeal,' he says. 'Most of our effort is trying to get the salespeople to leave us alone.' Cipes didn't always feel that way, though. Back in 2013, he was used to the routine. His conversion began when he e-mailed business-software maker Atlassian, asking the company to send him a sales rep, and it said no."

Atlassian's envious customer acquisition rate, you ask?

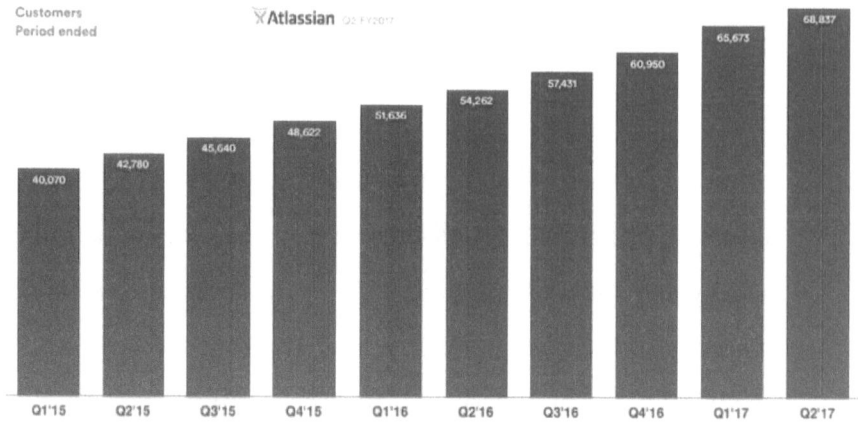

Customers: We define the number of customers at the end of any particular period as the number of organizations with unique domains that have at least one active and paid license or subscription of our products for which they paid more than $10 per month. While a single customer may have distinct departments, operating segments or subsidiaries with multiple active licenses or subscriptions of our products, if the product deployments share a unique domain name, we only include the customer once for purposes of calculating this metric. We define active licenses as those licenses that are under an active maintenance or subscription contract as of period end.

As for Sales and marketing costs as a percentage of revenue (from the same article):

When Less Is More
Sales and marketing costs as a percentage of revenue in the last 12 months

Company	Percentage
Atlassian	19%
Workday	37%
Salesforce.com	49%
ServiceNow	50%
NetSuite	52%
Marketo	60%
Box	80%

GRAPHIC BY BLOOMBERG BUSINESSWEEK; DATA: COMPILED BY BLOOMBERG

This chapter began with the question: Do you and your organization desire a market position where premium pricing, exceptional customer loyalty, robust job creation and remarkable PRG are the norm?

How do you feel about it now? When I deliver keynote speeches, and ask business audiences if they believe a monopoly can be formed within their respective industries, over 90% of hands shoot into the air – every time. For me, this has always caused a conundrum. If so many people believe a monopoly is possible, why don't more find out how to achieve it? The answer is simple, of course: *Change is hard.* "Good enough" is what most settle for. Many do not have the work ethic or intestinal fortitude to be successful with such a challenging endeavor, and even more do not have the right people in their organizations.

And this is why senior leadership should proceed with caution.

Chapter 15

Component Five:

Proceed With Caution

"Plan – Do – Check – Act"

~ Dr. W. Edwards Deming

"If the hypothesis is not confirmed and validated, then adoption is in jeopardy"

~ Sean Stormes

Legend John Wooden, UCLA's famous head basketball coach, often said as one of his many famous management principles, "Be quick, but don't hurry." Or you could go with what my grandmother used to tell me: "Haste makes waste." Choose your poison. Either way, the point is that there is danger in rushing to judgment with a Big Idea and its associated unprecedented value, assuming that you already know how customers will react. The good news is that there is also a failsafe to prevent against this danger. Ignore at your own risk.

Similar to a company's brand – where the customer owns it, not you – only the village can determine the degree of value an organization and its offerings provide. This validation phase is important insurance, protecting against potential and profit-eroding waste and rework. What is needed is a strong customer *endorsement*.

Key Points to Remember When Validating a Big Idea Hypothesis

If you need more proof for validating a Big Idea than the following statistics, I am not sure what to tell you:

"1,000 CEOs of small and midsize businesses were asked to name their top three competitive advantages. Their respective customers were then asked the same question. **997 CEOs got it wrong."** ~ 2011 SmartAdvantage® survey

"80% of CEOs said that their products were differentiated. **8% of consumers agreed."** ~ Bain and Company study

Four Compelling Reasons Why Customer-confirmation Is Warranted Before Launching Anything "New"

1. Your nascent offerings must be proven to be **super-relevant** to your Dream Customers – the MVV – or they are often worthless.

2. A significant amount of money – particularly in **sales and marketing** – could be wasted if this step is skipped. Remember, if it has to be "sold" or "advertised," it isn't good enough.

3. You do not own your brand. *Your customer does.* It is whatever they think it is, and is directly correlated to your brand reputation. Therefore, it is imperative to determine how you are **perceived**. Brand = What the organization stands for, and how that ideal is revealed to the MVV through its products, services and experiences.

4. Evidence of **co-creation**. Pay close attention to initial feedback. This is an excellent time to determine whether or not the MVV senses "co-destiny." The more ownership

customers have in your value proposition, the more loyal they become.

Questions That Need Answers

- What "Voice of the Customer (VOC)" vehicles are currently employed at your company?

  _____

  _____

- Where do your dream customers congregate? What "night clubs" do they frequent?

  _____

  _____

- What are your different methods of eavesdropping, and how can they be used to your advantage?

  _____

  _____

- How can you perform free customer research while simultaneously performing "unprecedented value" confirmation and validation?

_____

_____

> **Clean Slate Wisdom:** Ensure alignment between management perceptions and customer reality, or risk failure … and an enormous amount of waste and rework dollars. For these reasons, customer endorsement must be validated before marketing or selling activities occur.

Chapter 16

Component Six:

Captivation

"Marketing is not a department"

~ Jason Fried, Founder, Base Camp, and author of Rework

"Everything Communicates"

~ Sergio Zyman, Marketing Executive and author

"Leaders give people stories they can tell themselves; stories about future and about change."

~ Seth Godin

"Content informs. Stories inspire (and often compel action)."

~ Sean Stormes

If you must employ marketing, ensure it is of the "third millennium" variety. Marketing is the new selling – speaking, writing and other progressive tactics – but do not confuse those things with run of the mill "content management."

Rather, Third Millennium marketing involves:

1. **Dividing the marketplace.** Sound familiar? Pick a fight, professionally and tactfully. "This is who they are, and this is who we are." See the difference? Remember Apple's *I'm a Mac, I'm a PC* marketing campaign with

actor Justin Long? That is the approach to model – because it works.

2. **Thought leadership.** The objective is not to be a valued resource. The objective is to be THE source. Most are unwilling or unable to do it, which spells o-p-p-o-r-t-u-n-i-t-y for demand creators. Strive to both *elevate* and *own* the conversation.

3. **Making the village the hero.** It is not about you. It is about them, the customer! How will you ensure their success? How will you ensure they *win*?

4. **Telling emotional stories through the customer's lens, not yours.** What is the story people want to tell about *themselves*? How can you help them see and feel themselves in *that* story?

5. **Demand Creation.** Attraction!

> **Clean Slate Wisdom:** An organization's purpose statement is *not* a marketing slogan, and should never be represented as such. Rather, purpose should be "revealed" through a company's products, services and experiences. It should be "felt," not "told." Therefore, marketing efforts should reflect purpose without being literal.

Now That You Have Found Your "Voice" ...

Key Points to Remember:

- Your marketing and "unprecedented value" must align or risk customer confusion or apathy.

- Marketing efforts should position you as an industry authority, causing ideal clients to approach *you*. It should be strong enough to drive sales, not merely leads. Also, any education-based marketing should help clients achieve their goals, not yours.

- Another key objective is to build strong community, a sales force of rabid fans whose profound loyalty provides a never-ending stream of profitable opportunities (beyond leads). People seek an *emotional connection* strong enough to result in deep caring for you. Therefore, provide meaningful, beneficial events and regular communication.

- While websites, advertising and digital marketing are still relevant and effective, winning in the third millennium demands that we recognize our role as publishers of customer-beneficial content. This content should be delivered consistently via public speaking, writing and social media platforms.

Questions That Need Answers:

- How does your marketing partner – beyond traditional advertising – help you un-even the competitive playing field, allowing you to achieve marketplace distinction?

  _____
  _____

- What type of content are you providing, and to whom? Is about you, or them?

  _____
  _____

- How are you measuring your marketing activities? What are top management's expectations?

  _____
  _____

- If you are not an adequate writer, what options are at your disposal to help you achieve success?

  _____

  _____

- How do you ensure brand message consistency across every customer touch point?

  _____

  _____

Clean Slate Wisdom: The greatest marketing strategy ever devised is "*Care*." How do you care deeply, and often, about every single thing your company does, especially when designing an unprecedented value proposition born from seeing what others miss and unspoken customer needs? This leads us directly back to growth hacking – intentionally designing "Wow!" into offerings.

Section IV

Sustainability

Chapter 17

Ethnographer Rising:

The Salesperson's New Role

"I want to understand the world from your point of view, to know what you know in the way you know it. I want to understand the meaning of your experience,

to walk in your shoes, to feel things as you feel them, to explain things as you explain them. Will you become my teacher and help me understand?"

~ James P. Spradley, Professor of Anthropology, Macalester College

"You can't just ask customers what they want

and then try to give that to them.

By the time you get it built,

they'll want something new."

~ Steve Jobs, Apple Inc.

*"**Are you paying** salespeople to close sales (all about them and you), or to deliver new insights that can help create demand ...*

so you don't have to sell?"

~ Sean Stormes

A funny thing happens when senior leadership's primary goal is to intentionally design unprecedented value, driven from an elegant, resonant and meaningful purpose. They quickly connect the dots, realizing that the one group that possesses an all-inclusive V.I.P. pass to the customer is the *sales organization*. But if all they are tasked with is relentlessly driving sales, then they will not become obsessive about "seeing what others miss." There's a direct correlation between how people are compensated, and how they behave and what they ultimately deliver.

Sure, you could rely on your inner Elon Musk or Mark Zuckerberg – faux channeling existing visionaries who already possess Superman-like x-Ray vision, able to identify unprecedented value opportunities – but my guess is that if that person existed within you, then you would have already leveraged that DNA. Instead, coming back to reality, consider creating an army of:

- **Scouts.** In battle (and business *is* a type of battle), as Sun Tzu pointed out in *The Art of War*, it was the outlooks and spotters who were highly valued, honored and rewarded. Without these teams camped out on war zone periphery, constantly "seeing" and delivering a constant flow of valuable intelligence back to the generals, leaders would fly blind , victory much harder to achieve. Knowing important details in advance of battle is a primary tenet of demand creation.

- **Examiners.** These are curious sorts who derive excitement and high satisfaction from analysis, making unique observations heretofore undiscovered.

- **Sleuths.** When it's time to connect the disparate insights dots, these detectives are skilled at making sense of the menagerie that has been collected.

The harsh reality is that most existing salespeople will not be able to make the switch, especially those with lengthy tenure. Some old dogs might be able to learn new tricks, however more than likely you will have to blow up the sales organization and start over. While this may seem like a daunting proposition, consider the alternative – a non-purpose driven collection of "One-Through-Four" individuals (see Chapter 4, *Surrogate: The Only Reason the Sales Organization Exists – and it's not good*).

Please do not get me wrong, the old guard might still be fun – heck, invite them to parties! – however my advice is to steer clear of the career vagabond salesperson if your overarching objective is to create demand.

What Is Your Team's Critical Thinking Quotient?

How much time does your organization spend at the *front end* of the hiring process screening for and assessing critical thinking skills? And why are these skills integral to demand creation, and specifically the individuals formerly known as salespeople?

In 2012, Grant Tilus, who works for Collegis education and writes student-focused articles on behalf of Rasmussen College, assembled a list of six critical thinking skills aimed at helping prepare students for the business world (http://bit.ly/2sjxh0a):

Skill #1: Interpretation

What it Means: Having the ability to understand the information you are being presented with and being able to communicate the meaning of that information to others. Throughout your career you will be presented with a variety of information in many different types of situations. Imagine you are looking at demographic information, hoping to target a different group of customers for a new product. Interpretation skills will enable you to better decode the information and add clarity to what you have discovered – which in turn will help you better understand any potential new customer opportunities for your company.

Application Exercise: Write down 10 emotions you feel can be paired with facial expressions, e.g. smiling equals happiness. Then give your list to a friend and ask them to randomly recreate each facial expression as you attempt to interpret the correct emotion simply by looking at their face. You will learn how to identify the <u>key bits of information</u> you need in order to connect the dots. How many can you correctly identify?

Skill #2: Analysis

What it Means: Having the ability to connect pieces of information together in order to determine what the intended meaning of the information was meant to represent. Imagine you are reading a companywide memo that is discussing making changes in order to address recent movement within the business landscape. Having this skill will better provide you with the ability to "read between the lines" and help you understand how this will impact the overall strategy you have in your position.

Application Exercise: To practice this skill, try to determine the meaning behind this Chinese Proverb: "Be the first to the field and the last to the couch." Are you able to identify the intended meaning behind this statement? While we all analyze information a little differently, you should have been able to determine that this proverb is referencing having a hard work ethic.

Go here (https://www.upwork.com/leaving?ref=http%3A%2F%2Fwww.rasmussen.edu%2Fstudent-life%2Fblogs%2Fmain%2Fcritical-thinking-skills-you-need-to-master-now%2F) to practice some more in order to further develop this skill.

Skill #3: Inference

What it Means: Having the ability to understand and recognize what elements you will need in order to determine an accurate conclusion or hypothesis from the information you have at your disposal.

Picture yourself as a business manager; you are looking at the latest sales forecast and you see sales have decreased. It's important for you to be able to understand what additional information you may need in order to determine why that happened, including identifying internal issues, external competition or even economic conditions. The ability to understand the information you already have and determine what you may still need to find the best solution is an important skill for you to have no matter what career field you are in.

Application Exercise: Try watching an episode of a weekly crime show. Focus on absorbing the clues in an effort to determine the mystery of who completed the crime during the episode. These shows do a fantastic job of dropping clues and bits of information along the way that can help you make an educated guess prior to the end of the episode. Were you able to identify it correctly?

Skill #4: Evaluation

What it Means: Being able to evaluate the credibility of statements or descriptions of a person's experience, judgment or opinion in order to measure the validity of the information being presented.

Imagine you are leading a focus group at work to determine how your customers view the organization's products. You ask the group a few questions that uncover several negative opinions about certain items you sell. You will need to use this skill to evaluate those responses, so you can determine if the information you received is valid and whether or not it needs to be further looked into.

Application Exercise: With the invention of the Internet this is a skill you can hone anytime you begin a search online. For practice, run a search on how to be a leader at work to test your evaluation skills. Are you able to identify whether the information you find is reliable and valid? Being aware of additional information you may need to make this assessment is essential. (Hint: In this example, you may need to evaluate the website's URL, the author's bio and potentially many other pieces of information.)

Skill #5: Explanation

What it Means: Having the ability to not only restate information, but add clarity and perspective to the information, so it can be fully understood by anyone you are sharing it with. Imagine you are giving two presentations for new product ideas; one to the CEO of the company, and the other to product engineers. You know both groups are extremely interested in hearing what you have to say, but you will need to be able to explain these ideas in two very different ways. The CEO may only need to hear high level ideas about the products while the engineers will need more specific product details. Your ability to clearly explain your ideas while keeping in mind who you are presenting to is important for making sure the information is understood and well received.

Application Exercise: It's important to remember not everyone has or needs the knowledge or information you have. Practice this skill by explaining something complex that you have knowledge about to two different types of people. Use your kids and your spouse since they typically will not have the same level of knowledge of certain subjects. For example, explain to your kids and your spouse separately <u>how a cell phone works</u>. The explanation should be different since they have two different levels of knowledge yet both of them should receive a similar understanding of the subject.

Skill #6: Self-Regulation

What it Means: Having the awareness of your own thinking abilities and the elements that you are using to find results.

Imagine you are on the phone with a customer attempting to work through a problem they are having with your company's software, and it's your first week on the job. The problem they are having is complex, and yet, you still want to assist them in order to make a good impression at work. Your ability to understand that perhaps transferring them to a coworker with more knowledge on the subject is the best way to provide the customer with a positive result.

Application Exercise: It's important to be able to separate your own personal biases or self-interests when making decisions at work. Let's imagine your manager asks you to write down 10 reasons why you deserve a raise prior to an annual review. After you complete your reasons, read through each and *focus on identifying your own potential biases* that may impact your argument. Awareness of these biases will help you generate a much stronger case for getting a raise.

So the next time someone starts talking to you about developing critical thinking skills for your career, hopefully now you will be able to tell them you know what they are, how they are used in the workplace and how to go about continually developing them for the future.

Clean Slate Wisdom: How do you ensure that people in your organization can perform objective analysis of an issue, reason through ideas in a well thought manner, so that rational and effective judgments can be made? Training and assessments on this topic are directly correlated to successful demand creation and PRG.

Chapter 18

Reporting:

New Metrics, Measurements and Dashboards

"What gets measured gets managed, and what gets managed gets done"

~ Peter Drucker

"Measure the drivers of demand creation – the lead metrics – without ever losing sight of customer delight and profit, the two most accurate indicators of unprecedented value design"

~ Sean Stormes

As you might suspect, I have a different take on what should be measured in the demand creation Revenution. If a revenue revolution is your goal, then revolutionary metrics are required. While this chapter only offers what I've uncovered and recommend as of the writing of this book, it is not meant to be a comprehensive list. Each month I meet enlightened, Level 5 business leaders who open my eyes to new KPIs they are tracking, and therefore inspire me to constantly scout for new ways to report the drivers of demand creation.

The common theme, though, is that word: "drivers." The further up in the demand creation process you get, the better off you are. That is where valuable lead metrics reside.

Remember, traditional lag metrics are merely results. What you seek in the Revenution are the actions and behaviors that *drive* PRG results.

What To Measure

Customer delight. I give credit to my thoughts on this topic (and metric) to consultant Tom Peters of *In Search of Excellence* fame, among other best-selling books. Possessing a monthly quantitative measurement of customer satisfaction "provides a much better lead indicator of future organizational health than does profitability or market share change. We urge leadership to make the level of customer satisfaction the primary basis for incentive compensation and annual performance evaluation for virtually every person at every level in every function throughout the organization." Sage advice, indeed! How does your organization secure and measure the VOC (voice of the customer)? What is the formal methodology that tracks customer delight?

Key contributor retention. Without true champions – the organization's proven, top contributors – nothing good happens, and the hidden replacement costs not only erode profitability almost more than anything else, but also weaken the organization's value proposition and marketplace positioning. Once the village loses trust and confidence in the enterprise they love, the recovery incline is both mighty steep and costly. Therefore, invest heavily in your top people, including base salary. Is there a better place to overpay? I think not. Find the money by cutting non-contributors to demand creation and PRG. (NOTE: "Top people" are at all levels of the organization, not just management).

Customer attrition. Is there anything that causes more waste and rework than losing loyal, profitable customers? Too many companies focus on securing new business, when that it is far less costly to retain *existing* customers. Many in leadership cannot name their top ten attrition accounts, or the root causes for defection. If you seek PRG, almost nothing achieves results faster than plugging the gaping hole at the bottom of the sales funnel.

Observations, insights and new offerings. In Chapter 14, *Designing "Priceless,"* we learned about the Value Design Flow Map. Maps and diagrams serve an important purpose as visual aids for comprehending *concepts*, but they do nothing to enable action. Creating an observations and insights "warehouse" – where ethnography scouts can make their deliveries, and examiners and sleuths can perform analysis and study – is paramount to leveraging advance reporting so that unprecedented value can be forged.

Process Improvement. An organization is an ecosystem comprised of disparate processes that, once identified, understood, improved and optimized, will yield substantial results.

Training. Empowerment cannot occur until employees are able to make the same quality of decision that leadership does. Please hear me. I did not say "the same decisions as leadership." I said, "the same *quality* of decision." Suggested training topics to measure progress include:

- *Purpose.* Do people believe in the higher calling? How can assistance be provided?

- *Insights.* Observations are not insights, and seeing what others miss cannot be discovered with standard questioning. Heed the Value Design Flow Map, Chapter 14.

- *Design of unprecedented value.* "Incremental" is the enemy of "Unprecedented," therefore see the T3D Demand Creation Source Code diagram in Chapter 5.

- *Continuous Improvement.* I'm not referring to full blow Statistical Process Control or Lean or Total Quality Management training, at least for the first year. Rather, do people understand what a "system" is, and the plethora of related processes that make up that system? Is there a company ecosystem infographic depicting how the business machine should work in harmony – how the individual pieces make up the whole?

Determine How The Organization Generates The Most Profit, and Do More Of It

Surprisingly, most organizations are not aware of their greatest profit drivers. From what I have seen, most do not even know their customer segments and associated percentages relative to the whole. The 80/20 rule (Pareto Principle) is always evident, therefore most often 20% of a customer base or segment drives 80% of top line revenue. The same goes for where profit emanates from. Are the largest customers the most profitable (often they are not)? Those who place the largest orders? Is it the middle segment because they don't (can't) demand low pricing? Please consider: It's the *not knowing* that erodes the bottom line.

How can the purpose be fulfilled if there is not ample profit to fund it? Conversely, consider creating a list of "profit killers," and begin eradicating them immediately, starting with the greatest offenders. Then, identify Dream Customers who can contribute the most to your profit equation. Villages that are at the core of the unprecedented value offering are usually the most profitable. Said another way:

Rock solid customer belief, advocacy and delight =

Unprecedented profit

Chapter 19

Building the PRG All-Star Team: Organizational Chart Redesign

"Chiefs are not flawless decision makers. And the notion that 'people are everything' is incontestable. I nonetheless contend that top managers make lousy decisions and people fail to shine largely because burdensome structures and misaligned systems get in the way."

~ Tom Peters, Author and Management Consultant

"Your organization delivers the results it does because it is perfectly designed to do so"

~ Sean Stormes

Is your company structured properly to achieve the Attraction Model? As you have probably figured out, it is virtually impossible to achieve sustainable, revolutionary demand creation with a misaligned traditional organizational chart housing uninspired people with common (or worse) traits and abilities. To become a successful demand creator, senior leadership should stuff the company with transformational value architects who pine to join a meaningful movement. This is how to ensure important "fit," which takes priority over "smart." Then, the actual structure must be intentionally designed to allow unprecedented value design to flourish.

Implications of a Poor Organizational Structure

While demand creation is a worthwhile endeavor, what happens if the organization cannot effectively deliver on its unprecedented value proposition because of ineffective internal structure? Here are three important areas where inferior design can scorch even the best-intending businesses.

1. Short-term PRG.

Not only is immediate, top line revenue negatively impacted, but crucial pipeline opportunities are hurt, too. Throw in the inability to charge a premium because of perceived low value, and the profitable growth quilt begins to unravel. Also, please consider the impact within customer service. When substandard response time to important customer inquiries is evident, or orders delivered late become the norm, customers *will* leave. References are lost and the ability to attract new customers weakened. As revenue dwindles, making payroll becomes difficult, maintenance is put off, and the vicious downward spiral begins, so very hard to reverse.

2. Future Growth

New business does not magically appear on the doorstep. If plans are not made to create future opportunities, then PRG cannot be maximized. Without an organizational structure that regularly assembles key executives and employees for ideation (and other) purposes, it is near impossible to create effective long-term strategies. Therefore, strategic management includes engineering growth opportunities, such as introducing new products, services and experiences; forging new distribution channels; geographic expansion; or pursuing new target accounts or entire markets. These strategies often require input from multiple departments, including sales, marketing, purchasing, finance, operations and IT, and it is the owner's job to ensure the structure enables this requirement.

3. Increased Costs.

- *Productivity.* Unsound internal structure raises expenses due to inherent inefficiencies, thereby driving up labor costs necessary to perform the work. As an example, when the sales organization does not let operations management know about upcoming large orders, they cannot plan accordingly, leading to a lack of production capacity, labor availability, warehouse storage space and shipping efficiencies. Faulty organizational structure is directly correlated to the costly, damaging effects of waste and rework.

- *Centralized Decision-making.* Productivity can also suffer if the business structure remains centralized, particularly from a decision-making perspective. How can people act swiftly to make empowered decisions when they have to navigate a cumbersome managerial hierarchy designed to thwart them? Once again, it all comes back to purpose-driven, enlightened leadership who understand that ceding control actually makes them, and the organization far more powerful. If leadership desires better results, then the structure must be intelligently designed to deliver that outcome.

- *Employee Turnover.* Decentralized organizational structures can promote a competitive PRG strategy. Generally, small and mid-market businesses that cannot make the shift do not progress beyond the small business stage. Employees are most happy when engaged, and that engagement is the byproduct of nimble, ad hoc creative teams formed on a moment's notice (search "skunk works"), the result of a decentralized, aligned and clear organizational structure designed to foster such behavior. If morale isn't a strategic management objective, then costly employee churn will eventually occur. How does leadership ensure crisp, clear and consistent communication? How is creativity fostered, measured and realized? Without these organizational building blocks, critical opportunities could be missed, allowing problems to fester and reduce the aforementioned employee morale. Last, unhappy and disengaged people tend to not volunteer new ideas, and are more likely to jump ship. Once the organization's bad reputation seeps into the marketplace, finding and hiring top candidates becomes difficult. These types of candidates may feel their contributions would be wasted in a company where they would have no decision-making authority and see fewer opportunities for personal fulfillment.

Seven Employee Characteristics Required To Drive Faster Demand Creation

1. **See what others miss** (curious, empathetic and vulnerable; constantly identifying hassles)

2. **Critical thinking** (enjoy spending ample time with a particular problem)

3. **Take the initiative and embrace responsibility** (don't ask permission to tackle problems)

4. **Find their "voice"** (courage and high self-esteem)

5. **Communicate at a high level** (those who articulate well across channels win the day)

6. **Can get things done through others** (build consensus; collaborate; sell ideas; persuasive)

7. **Execute** *("There is no try, only do"* ~ Yoda, Star Wars; no excuses; welcome deadlines)

How Reflections Drive Demand Creation

The most important trait demand creators possess when confronted with "Where will tomorrow's demand come from?" is that they don't look to any of the Usual Suspects for clues or guidance. Rather, they look in the *mirror*. After all, what small and mid-market CEOs should seek to develop is a cumulative body of insight, not what a single genius can produce.

The Demand Creation Organization: Roles, Attributes and Responsibilities

- **CEO/Business Owner.** There can only be one top dog, and that person should possess the following attributes, including but not limited to –

    o *Humble and Willful/Resolute.* It is easy to find "resolute" because of the nature of the position – and therefore the individual – but humility is indeed a rare quality at the top. Elite CEOs must possess the courage to make the hardest of decisions, particularly when it comes to personnel, however compassion should often be a key consideration.

- *Visionary.* To be clear, a visionary is not an ideologue. The former can process market forces, trends and subtle nuances simultaneously, then place it all in a blender – sprinkling the knowledge with real life experience (so very important) and associated sage wisdom – employ just the right touch of ethnography, then take educated risks while outlining a clear plan to achieve the vision. On the other hand, an ideologue's conduct is guided more by the image of perfection than by the real world – often derived from the Usual Suspect Accepted Gurus. Theory devoid of practical experience is simply dreaming, and that cult-like state may be the most dangerous of all.

- *EQ.* Self-awareness, empathy, humility and vulnerability are just four "emotional intelligence" characteristics that are desirable for demand creation senior leadership. Combining EQ with data and experience helps leaders more effectively forge the necessary beliefs, thinking and behavior to win in the Revenution.

- *Commitment and obsession.* Steve Jobs was fanatical about design, simplicity and user experience that allowed Apple to become the most valuable company in the world. His hands on, take-no-prisoners behavior toward that true north philosophy willed the company forward while leaving anyone who was not on board in his wake. Harsh? *I think not.* Would you rather work for someone who is intolerant of those who are not willing to help fulfill the purpose, mission and vision – someone whom you know unequivocally what they stand for – or a senior leader whose compass moves by the week, influenced by seasonal winds?

- *Sentient.* Self-awareness is crucial to holding top company positions, however just being "aware" of surroundings – being in the moment – may be the most valuable state to aspire to. Possessing sensitivity while remaining resolute toward fulfillment of purpose, mission and vision only enhances demand creation results.

- **Human Resources**. Policies and procedures should center around the three primary focuses of this book: Continuous improvement, the constant rooting out of costly waste and rework; Organizational fitness, forging a culture of Purpose and Core Behaviors; and Demand creation, the Seven Steps of PRG. Chapter 20, *Full Integration: Baking the New Model Into the Company's Bones*, outlines how to perform effective organizational integration.

- **Sales and Marketing**. First things first. I recommend that Sales, Marketing and Customer Service report to the same leader. R&D (Sales) and Captivation (marketing) should merge into a singular, powerful force. Since most mid-market companies do not have the luxury of a traditional R&D department, the ethnographers (formerly salespeople) will have to do – and if you have the right scouts, they will do a formidable job.

- **Operations/Production**. Is there a customer-centric, continuous improvement, Level Five-type leader at the helm? While marketing is not a department, neither is "sales." Every aspect of an organization is a customer touch point, part of the value proposition ecosystem, and therefore a key component that contributes to, or damages the organization's demand creation efforts.

- **Finance.** Is there a growth budget, i.e. a PRG/demand creation budget? How about a margin improvement plan, directly correlated to creating demand?

- **New roles, as needed**. How often are employees asked about their dream job? How often do those dreams come true? While employees often do not have the power to change company systems, they do know where the problems are, and that makes them uniquely qualified to design roles their most passionate about and qualified for.

A Few Notes On Actual Structure

While I am frequently asked to provide the perfect, one-size-fits-all template for organizational structure, no such thing exists. Rather, let us begin with common sense.

As previously mentioned, are sales, marketing and customer service aligned under a singular leader? This is the "customer" bucket. How about the "product" bucket, or "people" or "procurement" buckets? Identify natural groupings and coordinate accordingly. Additionally, seek to break down barriers between departments by aligning (structuring) them more closely, when possible. The 25% to 40% (or more) you are wasting in waste and rework will thank you.

Additionally, consider forming a Navy Seal Team Six-type, Special Ops Forces unit to handle the firm's toughest missions, be they internal or external (customer issues). I have personally assembled such teams, and the ROI is significant. These small units, usually five people or less, often consist of masters in the areas of creativity, vision, continuous improvement, strong institutional knowledge and above all else, *execution*. For maximum results, be sure to grant full autonomy coupled with uncommon humility and collaboration skills. Allow them to form their charter and pick their projects, reporting as needed to ownership. And don't forget to reward them handsomely.

Another recommendation is to ask employees:

- "How does our organizational structure …
    - "prevent you/us from delighting customers?"
    - "cause waste and rework?"

- "cost us too much time to make decisions?"
- "hamper clear communication?"

In conclusion, what parts of the current structure are not adding value, and therefore most likely need to go, or the people redeployed into more valuable roles that fulfill purpose, drive demand and delight customers? While these are always hard decisions, that is the domain and behavior of CEOs and business owners in the Revenution.

Chapter 20

Full Integration:

Baking the New Model Into The Company's Bones

"We believe that it's really important to come up with core values that you can commit to, meaning that you're willing to hire and fire based on them."

~ Tony Hsieh, CEO, Zappos

"Determine what behaviors and beliefs you value as a company, and have everyone live true to them. These behaviors and beliefs should be so essential to your core that you don't even think of it as culture."

~ Brittany Foryth, VP of Human Relations, Shopify

"If you desire significant PRG, then prove to all stakeholders that you stand for something more, something meaningful"

~ Sean Stormes

Commitment. Essential. Meaningful. The above quotes invoke bold language, and justifiably so. If the ingredients to PRG success are peripheral to each employee's daily expectations and duties, then demand creation nirvana is nothing but a pipe dream. People accomplish not only what they are paid to do, they are also inspired to perform based on how the company values them related to living the purpose, core behaviors and other key components contained in this book.

Sustainability:
Designing the Organization's "Baked Goods"

The final step in ensuring organizational fitness is making the desired and necessary demand creation behaviors integral to how the company does business. Here is a list, by department, of what needs to occur.

For each of the roles below, sustainability and success will only occur if leaders (and others) are held accountable to the associated tactics (directly underneath each role):

- Process
- Responsibility (who)
- PRG Components
- Execution
- Integrated (who does what by when)

Sustainability by Department

Senior Management

- Sense of Purpose
- Competitive Advantage Strategy
- Management Meetings
- Company Communications
- Reporting
- Goal Development
- Innovation (new product, service and experience development)
- Customer Experience (internal and external)
- Build Customer Community

Human Resources

- Job Descriptions
- Employee Development (personal growth)
- Reviews (quarterly and annual)
- Compensation
- Hiring
- Progressive Discipline

- Termination
- Promotion
- Reward and Recognition

Sales

- Define and Identify Dream Client
- R&D (ethnography; customer research)
- Observations and insights collected/shared
- Metrics, measurements and dashboards
- Daily/Weekly activities (<u>drivers</u> of PRG)

Marketing

- Positioning (ensuring alignment around all customer touch points)
- Connecting the "insights dots"
- Help Sales "sell the problem" (not solutions)
- Customer education
- Writing (Story: The customer as hero)
- Public Speaking (by leadership and others)

Operations

- Meet or exceed internal and external customer experience expectations
- Observations and insights collected/shared

Finance

- Customer-centric policies and procedures
- Observations and insights collected/shared

Procurement/Purchasing

- Ensure suppliers believe in, and help fulfill the organization's purpose
- Observations and insights collected/shared

Chapter 21

Cold Turkey:

Seven PRG-destroying Activities To Cease Immediately

"You know you got to go through hell

Before you get to heaven"

~ Steve Miller Band,
Jet Airliner

"Wake up and smell the future,

because it's been here for a while"

~ Sean Stormes

If you think you are ready to take the plunge into a genuine, *Clean Slate* world, then it is best to rip off the Band-Aid quickly. But if cessation is not your thing, then be prepared for a miserable life in purgatory, because heaven will not be within reach. Denial, unfortunately, is one of business's most deadly sins, yet it is far more prevalent than what you might suspect.

With all of this in mind, and possessing an ample amount of intestinal fortitude, see how much of the following you can bite off before next Monday arrives.

Clean Slate-Aspiring Leaders Need To Stop ...

1. Mistaking Mission for Purpose. First, your mission is probably milquetoast, weak and non-inspiring in so many ways. Second, the mission is "the core strategy that fulfills the purpose." No purpose, no mission. Third, purpose is intended to be relentlessly chased – never to be fully achieved – yet no so far into the future that it's unreasonable and demotivating to the organization.

2. Believing that your business possesses real competitive advantage. At best, you might have strengths or differentiation, and neither will do much for you in the quest to un-even your competitive playing field. What you seek is unprecedented value, derived from an organizational culture obsessed with seeing what others miss.

3. Believing that you – the business owner or CEO – knows what customers value most. Even if you are an evolved, emotional intelligence-type leader, you are probably not asking customers the right questions that could uncover unprecedented value. Besides, who in the organization is going to tell the boss she's full of crap – that she doesn't have a clue? Better idea: Ask customer-facing employees their thoughts and opinions, and commission some customer research. Last, employ bi-annual fact-finding missions with the 20% of customers who drive 80% of your business. And while you are at it, perform the same mission with your competitors' top customers, humbly asking them for input on how your company, and industry, can improve.

4. Assuming that you have the "right" people, and that success is merely a function of getting them "in the right seats on the bus." Name a business guru, and almost all of them skip over this most important fact, and – based on my experience – this is the primary reason why business owners often lament, "Yeah, I tried that. It didn't work." An engine cannot run at peak efficiency if it is made with substandard parts, and assembled in a shoddy manner. In fact, on a somewhat related note, most everyone in the company knows of the one person that needs to go, and they are (impatiently) waiting on you to do the right thing and terminate them.

5. Relying on the Sales force for PRG. Salespeople did not design your hollow value proposition (the founder/owner/CEO/leadership team did), and yet now they are doomed to a life of "Hit your numbers, or else!" To make matters worse, the customer is now in charge of identifying real value, not the traditional salesperson. Do you have people who are expert at seeing what others miss, and can ask intelligent, challenging questions? Or do you have "sellers," driven by selfish commission structures solely based on revenue volume? If you have the latter, welcome to perpetual frustration, turnover and incremental growth at best.

6. Thinking, "Waste and rework isn't a problem at my company." Bullshit! There is no line item on the P&L for waste and rework because it has not been identified and named, and therefore cannot be measured. If something is not measured, then it cannot be managed for improvement. That is because W&R is buried deep inside your company's systems and processes. It is the hidden, silent killer. Nothing improves profitability faster than reducing organizational variation.

7. Making decisions so damn complicated. Regardless of the size or scope of decision, only one question needs to be asked: "Does it help fulfill the purpose?" If it does, move forward. If it does not, then move on to something that does. A side benefit of this type of decision-making is that meeting time can be reduced dramatically. Additionally, other expenses – caused by variation and pesky waste and rework – can also be decreased because both organizational alignment and clarity are increased.

Appendix "A"

Deming's 14 Points For Management, Revenution Style

In the Revenution, progressive business leaders embrace and encourage behaviors that include design thinking, values-based strategy development, individual expression and creativity, the challenging of authority and the status quo, and long-term thinking as viable competitive sales weapons.

If you have never heard of, or read Deming's 14 Points For Management, please do yourself a favor before proceeding. Spend 20 minutes online examining the master's concepts and impact on industry. If this is your first exposure without appropriate context and perspective, you might experience brain freeze similar to downing half an ICEE in a single gulp.

Deming spent a good portion of his life developing the 14 Points, which first appeared in his magnum opus, *Out of the Crisis*, originally published in 1982. It was so counterintuitive to traditional American management philosophy (and a bit academic) that many rejected it. However, to those who adopted the new philosophy, executed, and achieved the intended transformation, their companies have never been the same: Ford Motor Company, Proctor and Gamble, and Xerox to name just three.

In fact, the leaders of Ford and Xerox directly credit Dr. Deming with saving their companies from certain extinction. For example, in 1980 Ford was losing $1.5 billion per year and had the worst reputation for quality and reliability of any American car company. Today, Ford is both the highest quality American car maker and the most profitable, and they are poised to overtake GM as the largest American automobile maker for the first time in almost seventy years. This has not happened by accident, and Deming is often cited as the reason. Additionally, a 1991 U.S. News & World Report cover story named Deming's contribution to the world as one of only nine "Hidden Turning Points in World History," along with events including Columbus' discovery of America and Napoleon's conquest of Europe.[6] That's lofty company.

The direct application of Dr. Deming's renowned 14 Points to the Revenution requires interpretation using core components that we will learn about later. Do not fret,

---

[6] *The Power of TRUE Quality Management*, January 2012, Matthew Cross, President of Leadership Alliance

though, as we are not getting ahead of ourselves. Much like Deming's philosophy, the Revenution takes time to digest, contemplate and understand. Therefore, continuous exposure serves to accelerate comprehension. It will all make sense, over time, if your goal is to succeed in a business development world that currently resides in illusions and misperceptions.

While it took Deming 70 years to cultivate and clearly articulate his 14 Points, it will only take you a day or two to grasp because of the logic involved. However, putting the 14 Points to use takes patience and skill.

Origin of Deming's 14 Points For Management

Dr. Deming said:

"The 14 points are the basis for transformation of American industry. It will not suffice merely to solve problems, big or little. Adoption and action on the 14 points are a signal that the management intends to stay in business and aims to protect investors and jobs.

"Such a system formed the basis for lessons for top management in Japan in 1950 and in subsequent years. The 14 points apply anywhere, to small organizations as well as to large ones, to the service industry as well as to manufacturing. They apply to a division within a company."

1. *"Create constancy of purpose toward improvement of product and service, with the aim to become competitive and to stay in business, and to provide jobs."*

   ➢ **Revenution Application:** Defeat sameness. Implement an effective and sustainable PRG process rooted in designing real customer demand. Eschew traditional sales models and weak value propositions that rely on manipulative salesperson techniques and a win-lose selling scenario.

2. *"Adopt the new philosophy. We are in a new economic age. Western management must awaken to the challenge, must learn their responsibilities, and take on leadership for change."*

   ➢ **Revenution Application:** Top management must create constant customer demand for its company's products and services, thereby putting everyone in the company into a position to win. They must lead by example, beyond lip service. Leadership's commitment to the new philosophy should be evident, approving necessary design changes to existing processes that prevent meaningful PRG from occurring.

3. *"Cease dependence on inspection to achieve quality. Eliminate the need for inspection on a mass basis by building quality into the product in the first place."*

   ➢ **Revenution Application:** To reduce or eliminate costly waste and rework that commonly occurs near the end of the sales process – like overcoming price objections and buyer's remorse – focus improvement efforts at the front end of the process. Sales-related problems are caused by factors that can often be eliminated once identified and quantified.

4. *"End the practice of awarding business on the basis of price tag. Instead, minimize total cost. Move toward a single supplier for any one item, on a long-term relationship of loyalty and trust."*

   ➢ **Revenution Application:** Customers will pay more if they receive more in return. Design the price/benefit value proposition to be unprecedented and irresistible.

Choose dream clients based on a carefully developed, intentional set of desirable traits. Long-term customer (and employee) retention is far more valuable than low-margin volume and short-term wins intended to pad sales numbers. Less is more.

5. *"Improve constantly and forever the system of production and service, to improve quality and productivity, and thus constantly decrease costs."*

> ➢ **Revenution Application:** See Point #3. Additionally, stop doing the same things harder and expecting different results. The current business development model is broken and in dire need of replacement. Once the new PRG system is in place, commit to ongoing sales process improvement. As the process becomes more efficient, key metrics will improve, including sales conversion ratios, customer demand, and customer loyalty.

6. *"Institute training on the job."*

> ➢ **Revenution Application:** Beyond product knowledge, provide education that enhances empathy,

curiosity, critical thinking and the PRG process. Train everyone on continuous process improvement methods. Instead of traditional skills and traits, hire employees (not just salespeople) with the following attributes in mind: Listening, ideation, creativity, writing, speaking, and problem solving. Also seek curiosity, adaptability, and empathy. Most training should occur within these disciplines as they relate directly to improved PRG.

7. *"Institute leadership. The aim of supervision should be to help people and machines and gadgets to do a better job. Supervision of management is in need of overhaul, as well as supervision of production workers."*

> ➢ **Revenution Application:** Replace dictators with teachers and mentors who help others optimize systems and processes. The company should replace a "selling" mindset with an ethos of "helping." Implement the internal customer concept, where each person who uses the previous person's work creates a set of requirements that must be fulfilled. Externally, the goal is to help customers achieve their specific

company goals, and most often, their customer's goals. Leaders in the Revenution are rewarded for helping others succeed.

8. *"Drive out fear so that everyone may work effectively for the company."*

   > **Revenution Application:** Determine what is causing fear and eliminate it as quickly as possible. Fear, forged by leadership, is responsible for lack of innovation and waste and rework, including securing unprofitable accounts, falsifying reports, and selling on price. Fear is a cancer that prevents most companies from achieving optimum results.

9. *"Break down barriers between departments. People in research, design, sales, and production must work as a team, to foresee problems of production and in use that may be encountered with the product or service."*

   > **Revenution Application:** Align the key components of the PRG ecosystem that traditionally operate independently into a system of steps that must be performed in order to realize maximum results (see

Chapter 3). A redesign of the organizational chart – including associated systems and processes – is required for success (see Point 12).

10. *"Eliminate slogans, exhortations, and targets for the work force asking for zero defects and new levels of productivity. Such exhortations only create adversarial relationships, as the bulk of the causes of low quality and low productivity belong to the system and thus lie beyond the power of the work force."*

    - *"Eliminate work standards (quotas) on the factory floor. Substitute leadership."*

    - *"Eliminate management by objective. Eliminate management by numbers, numerical goals. Substitute leadership."*

    ➢ **Revenution Application:** In the above bullet points, "substitute leadership" means employing statistical theory ("profound knowledge," in Deming's words), specifically to recognize the difference between common and special causes, and how each effects process performance. Goal setting, for example, is grounded in guesswork, not statistical fact. Similarly, numerical quotas do nothing to enhance the PRG system, nor are they a true indication of individual ability. Measuring the real drivers of PRG, using profound knowledge, is the only proven method of enhancing performance. 90% of all mistakes, errors, and problems are caused by the system, not the employee. Therefore, improve the PRG process to achieve the level of performance you seek. Once the origin of errors is identified within the system, people will work together to solve them because the individual is no longer blamed.

11. *"Remove barriers that rob the hourly worker of his right to pride of workmanship. The responsibility of supervisors must be changed from sheer numbers to quality."*

> **Revenution Application:** Review Points 7 through 10. Understand that the systems and processes that management created prevent people from achieving maximum job performance. Ask people why mistakes occur, and they will tell you (as long as fear is not present). Then, admit that front-line workers possess enormous insight into the company's processes, and customers, and therefore must be involved in any

discussions about value proposition design. Front-line workers and middle management may not have all of the answers, but they do know which questions to ask. Make employees true partners in PRG design, and help them succeed.

12. *"Remove barriers that rob people in management and in engineering of their right to pride of workmanship. This means the abolishment of the annual or merit rating and of management by objective."*

> **Revenution Application:** Review Point #10 regarding the dangers of MBO. Also, develop more intelligent architecture for assessing pay raises and promotions. The current model is generally flawed and unfair, leaving the employee at the mercy of unrealistic numerical goals, random variation outside their control, and substandard leadership. High-performing salespeople are often (still) promoted to sales management positions, though unqualified to lead others, while potential leaders are left behind. Implement a new set of desirable, Revenution-related attributes directly related to optimizing PRG performance, and measure subjectively.

13. *"Institute a vigorous program of education and self-improvement."*

> **Revenution Application:** Review Point #6. Additionally, realize that any education is valuable, even if it is not directly related to the employee's job function. The learning organization possesses one of the world's foremost competitive advantages: the ability to acquire knowledge faster than its competitors.

14. *"Put everybody in the company to work to accomplish the transformation. The transformation is everybody's job."*

> **Revenution Application:** A company's PRG infrastructure (its business development systems and processes) must be optimally aligned to achieve maximum efficiency and results. Leadership must first know what to do, then ensure that everyone in the company knows what to do, and how to do it. Leadership must be more than supportive since it is the engine that transforms the company.

About the Author

Sean Stormes leads The Third Door, a profitable revenue growth strategy firm. A nationally recognized authority on helping progressive leadership design, develop and deliver purpose-driven business models that create strong marketplace demand, he founded his company after a distinguished 27-year executive career rooted in key growth areas including Innovation, Continuous Improvement, Sales, and Marketing.

Sean is a published author, sought after keynote speaker and a former nationally syndicated guest columnist to the American City Business Journals, reaching thousands of business leaders across 43 top U.S. markets each year. More helpful content can be found at SeanStormes.com.

CONNECT WITH SEAN STORMES!

WWW.SEANSTORMES.COM

How *Purpose* Ignites Profitable Growth

Sean is available to speak in-person with your group! He delivers compelling presentations for your:

- ❖ Keynote
- ❖ Breakout Session
- ❖ Workshop

On the website, click "Invite Sean to Speak" for more details!

 T3DRevenution

 @SeanStormes

www.ingramcontent.com/pod-product-compliance
Lightning Source LLC
Chambersburg PA
CBHW020628220526
45464CB00001B/67